THE PUBLIC ADMINISTRATION CASEBOOK

Robert A. Cropf
St. Louis University

Jennifer M. Giancola
St. Louis University

Kirsten Kim Loutzenhiser
Troy University

Routledge
Taylor & Francis Group

LONDON AND NEW YORK

First published 2012 by Pearson Education, Inc.

Published 2016 by Routledge
2 Park Square, Milton Park, Abingdon, Oxon OX14 4RN
711 Third Avenue, New York, NY 10017, USA

Routledge is an imprint of the Taylor & Francis Group, an informa business

ISBN: 9780205607419 (pbk)

Cover Designer: Suzanne Behnke

Library of Congress Cataloging-in-Publication Data
Cropf, Robert A.
   The public administration casebook/Robert Cropf, Jennifer M. Giancola,
   Kirsten Kim Loutzenhiser
      p. cm.
   Includes bibliographical references and index.
   ISBN-13: 978-0-205-60741-9 (alk. paper)
   ISBN-10: 0-205-60741-1 (alk. paper)
      1. Public administration—United States—Case studies.   2. Social action—
   United States—Case Studies.   3. Social policy—United States—Case Studies
   I. Giancola, Jennifer M.   II. Title.
JK421.C77 2012
351.73—dc22
                                                                      2010053147

CONTENTS

THEMATIC CONTENTS

STRATEGIC MANAGEMENT

DEMOCRACY

PRIVATIZATION

REFORM

INTRODUCTION

OBJECTIVES AND OVERVIEW

Public policy, public administration, and, more generally, public service are showing renewed growth and vitality in terms of both educational and career opportunities. This is happening despite the continuing uncertainty regarding the economy and the restructuring of entire industrial sectors, including automobile manufacturing and finance. Indeed, issues associated with globalization, the environment, terrorism, immigration, and the economy all point to the importance of public policy and public administration in helping to find practicable solutions. Given the current political environment, it is critical that public service professionals are well prepared to tackle these and other key issues. Not only does this require the proper academic training, but it also demands extensive practice-based knowledge and skills. Much of the responsibility falls on public affairs/administration faculty and programs to better prepare practitioners.

Not only do students need better preparation for the public service, but the profile of these students is also rapidly changing with an increase of in-service, diverse, and nontraditional students including more females, part-time students, students attending two-year institutions, first-generation students, working adults, and students with one or more dependents (Choy, 2002; U.S. Department of Education, 2002). These trends are radically altering the face of higher education and, in particular, public administration programs (Loutzenhiser & Orman, 2005). Thus, there is an ongoing need for public administration programs to use teaching methods geared toward adult learners and other nontraditional students—methods referred to in the scholarly literature as *andragogy* (Knowles, 1988; Merriam & Caffarella, 1999). Andragogy attempts to facilitate more effective adult learning by integrating more of the learner's lived experience into the learning process. For these nontraditional students, pedagogical techniques that incorporate subject matter that relates directly to the their lives and is problem oriented as opposed to theoretical is the preferred method.

Why and for Whom Was the Book Written?

Dialogue with colleagues and professionals from the National Association of School of Public Affairs and Administration (NASPAA) led the authors to conclude that there is a need to meet the educational and professional requirements of a new generation of students in public administration undergraduate and graduate programs. A number of ideas were discussed for meeting these needs, including one that gave rise to this project—a book of real-life case studies written with working adults in mind. The case study method is one way to better meet the educational requirements of a wide range of students because the orientation of many of today's students tends to be more practice based and less theoretical in nature. Therefore, current learners appreciate efforts to bridge the gap between theory and practice. Although this is essential to any student of public administration (Reid & Miller, 1997), it is particularly salient for current students. However, there is a lack of texts that "speak to" the lived experience of students, ones that provide them with meaningful and relevant examples drawn from those experiences.

At the time of these discussions, a book such as this one did not exist. Thus, this book was written in order to provide students with applied examples incorporating workforce-relevant issues into the curriculum (White, 2004). This volume is the direct result of that discussion as well as subsequent conversations and other collaborations involving the authors. The case material contained herein is geared toward preparing students to become effective practitioners in the public and nonprofit sectors. The cases are written and compiled in such a way that they are all practice based and appeal to a variety of consumers, including traditional and nontraditional students. The book is designed to serve either as a companion to current introductory public administration textbooks or as a stand-alone casebook.

Unique Features of the Book

Another unique aspect of this casebook is that all the third authors of the cases were students. The cases are based on their actual experiences in organizational settings (see the later section on Casebook Methodology for additional information). A result of our students' deep involvement in the creation, development, and writing of each of these case studies is that the material better reflects current workplace realities and therefore results in a more meaningful learning experience for everyone. Specifically, the value of this approach is that it

- Enhances pedagogy by providing a means for students to become deeply immersed in the learning process
- Provides a teaching case methodology that serves as an easily adaptable model for other instructors
- Stimulates more interest in the public administration issues and theories discussed in class: when students analyze the cases, they can see their direct relevance to actual workplace experience
- Focuses on everyday people in ordinary situations as opposed to unique situations or national figures as other cases in the literature have done
- Provides an opportunity for student writers to reflect on their own experience and tie it in with the material covered in class
- Offers a text that speaks to the real-life experiences of students and, in particular, in-service and nontraditional students

The cases were all written in conjunction with students in the following programs:

- Working adult students in Saint Louis University's School for Professional Studies, specifically senior-level nontraditional students in the organizational studies, criminal justice, and public administration undergraduate programs

- In-service and masters-level students in Saint Louis University's Masters of Public Administration (MPA) program

The following types of students will derive the most benefit from the cases:

- Upper-level undergraduate students taking an introductory course in public administration
- First-year students in an MPA or similar degree program taking the required introductory course in public administration
- In-service, diverse, and nontraditional students in undergraduate- and graduate-level public administration or nonprofit management programs

The Themes of the Cases

Most of the significant themes covered in a typical introductory public administration course are included in this casebook. The complete list of themes is shown in Table 1. Since the choice of case study subject matter

TABLE 1   Thematic Content of the Case Studies

Case Name	Main Themes	Secondary Theme(s)
Oakdale Administrator	Decision making, financial management	Political context, ethics
Crime Victim Support Center	Decision making	Ethics, bureaucracy
ReadNow!	Decision making, ethics	Communication, intergovernmental affairs
Community Credit Union	Social equity, implementation/ evaluation	Financial management
Southern Medical School	Bureaucracy, ethics	Organizational culture
Stoughton City Budget	Financial management, bureaucracy and structure	Leadership, strategic management
University Phone Center	Leadership , HR administration	Organizational culture
Grassroots Change Initiative, Inc.	Decision-making, implementation/evaluation	Democracy, privatization
Social Security Administration	Bureaucracy and structure, HR administration	Intergovernmental affairs, ethics
Holy Spirit Church Bookkeeper	Decision making, bureaucracy and structure	Ethics, financial management

(continued)

TABLE 1 Continued		
Case Name	**Main Themes**	**Secondary Theme(s)**
Rio Estrecho Authority	Bureaucracy and structure, decision making	Political context, intergovernmental relations
U.S. Coast Guard	Leadership, bureaucracy and structure	HR administration, organizational culture
Islamic Center	Implementation, planning	HR administration, leadership
Community Health Center	Planning, strategic management	Reform, organizational culture

was left entirely up to the students, perhaps it is not surprising that certain themes are more salient than others. Decision making, bureaucracy and organizational structure, leadership, human resource administration, and professional and personal ethics stand out in particular as the themes most written about by the students in their cases. Arguably, these are the aspects of organizational life that most impact working students, at least as far as our sample is concerned. Other important themes covered by the cases include organizational culture, fiscal management, privatization, and organizational communication. Several of our cases involve nonprofits, reflecting the reality that many MPAs are employed by this sector, a trend that will continue well into the future. An intriguing aspect of these nonprofit cases is that they allowed us to broaden the scope of topics to cover faith-based and grassroots citizens' organizations, which are not typically included in standard public administration textbooks. Again, a strong case can be made that the choice of subject matter in these case studies reflects the altered landscape facing current MPAs, who now have direct experience with the increasing significance of nongovernmental organizations (NGOs) in public service delivery.

The Student Coauthors and the Writing Process

The contents of this book reflect the best examples of student-written case studies collected over a two-year period and selected from more than forty such assignments. Thus, for every case included, more than two other cases were deemed unsuitable. All the cases were written by students from two different courses: an introductory course in public administration at the graduate level (taught by one of the lead authors) and a senior-level undergraduate organizational theory and practice course. In the case of the latter, the students were either juniors or seniors and were predominantly "adult learners"—that is, people with full-time jobs and usually families and who are working on their bachelor's degrees. In addition, the graduate students tended to be largely employed in full-time or part-time jobs, although there were a small number of individuals who came into the MPA program straight from undergraduate programs.

Students in both courses were given essentially the same assignment: to write a case study based on their experience in a work setting. They were asked to follow the method for writing cases described in the next section (also see Case Study Assignment in the Appendix for an example of an actual assignment). As might be expected, the quality of the students' work varied widely. In most cases, however, their products were thoughtful exercises in which they had the opportunity to reflect on a workplace experience and distill from it a meaningful lesson, which they then shared with the class. In a couple of instances, one of the professors was told that the process had produced a dramatic effect; the two student-writers used terms such as "unique," "creative," and "enlightening" in describing the effect the assignment had on them. However, it should also be noted that there were other students who found the assignment to be somewhat frustrating because it took them out of their comfort zone. This reflects the unfortunate fact that most students, either at the undergraduate or graduate level, seldom have any real opportunities to integrate their workplace realities with their education, which contributes to the compartmentalization of their classroom learning from their working life. It also leads to the marginalization of their lived experience such that it becomes something not serious enough to be discussed in class. The case method, as it was used in this book, reverses this equation: one's work experience is reflected on and written about, as well as discussed in class. It is advisable that instructors, who wish to use the case method, work very closely with students as they prepare their cases. With this strategy in mind, we broke the entire assignment into several parts and required drafts for each part before the final product was due. This allowed for feedback to be given to the students on a regular basis. As a result of this method, students developed more confidence in themselves and the end result was a better product.

After students submitted their cases, these were carefully vetted by both of the lead authors. The criteria for selection included relevance (i.e., did it include at least one of the public administration course themes?) and readability. The case had to "grab the reader's interest" in some way. Another important concern was whether the case "spoke" to the experience of the typical student/worker. As they were all based on the lived experiences of real people, this criterion was easily met. After the initial selections, the student case writers were notified that their work was being considered for this book (students were also informed that their case assignments might be included in a book at the beginning of the course). Most were excited by the prospect of publication of their work. The cases were then divided between the two main authors, who had the task of making the material ready for publication.

CASE STUDY METHODOLOGY

The case method is a proven pedagogical technique in the training of professionals, with a history stretching back to the ancient Greeks and the so-called Socratic method (Lynn, 1999). For example, medical schools, law schools, business schools, and schools of social work all use teaching cases as an important component in the training of professionals. Public administration is no exception; two notable examples include Harvard's Kennedy School, which maintains a large number of teaching cases, and more recently, the University of Washington's Electronic Hallway, which provides an online database that anyone can access after registering. Even though the case method is quite familiar to many public administration programs, this casebook is unique in that it uses student-written cases instead of the more traditional case studies based on historical events and written by academics.

Objectives

The appeal of using student-written cases to train professionals is easy to understand. The cases provide an ideal vehicle for students to personally apply the theories and concepts taught in the classroom to the solution of real organizational problems. This happens in several ways . First, writing cases forces students to reflect on some work experience (theirs or someone else's) in a manner that informs professional practice by integrating classroom concepts, critically analyzing the situation and key issues, and exercising their problem-solving skills in developing the case. Students use these important skills initially in the case-writing process and then as leaders of a group discussion of the case. In leading the discussion, student-writers are placed in the position of acknowledging the multiple viewpoints and perspectives that fellow group members bring to a problem, ideas that might not have been apparent to the case writers as they were developing the case. Furthermore, exposure to multiple points of view teaches students to recognize that for some problems there may be many possible solutions.

Second, writing cases provides an opportunity for students to gain through the classroom what others acquire only through previous (sometimes considerable) job experience. When preprofessional students have yet to enter the work world, working on cases allows them to simulate the kinds of situations they might encounter at some point during their careers. In other words, the case study approach accommodates both the in-service and the pre-service student, without presenting an andragogical problem to either type of student. The andragogical approach is inclusive, and this turns some distinctions on their head, such as the in-service/pre-service dilemma on how to approach students. Indeed, a key premise of our model is that the cases are produced by experience and reproduced to allow for a knowledge exchange. This bridging of theory and practice makes theory relevant in a way that motivates both traditional and nontraditional students. The average student can relate to cases that come from the everyday world, whereas case studies of major national events involving important figures are so far removed from their daily experience that they can seem like theory to students.

Finally, the case-writing method is a pedagogical tool that appropriately serves diverse audiences. Student-writers do not need any special educational backgrounds to immediately delve into developing cases and leading the group discussion. Cases can be used equally effectively in college classrooms and government training programs. There is no "average" or typical case user; one can find pre-service students and experienced administrators preparing and discussing cases. The only difference is in the richness of experiential background that each will bring to the integration of theory and practice. This supports adult learning and suggests that the student is transformed in the learning environment through the in-class exchange.

Stages of Case Study Writing

There are four major stages involved in the creation of a typical case: developing a case outline, writing a case prospectus, conducting research, and writing the case. In addition, after the case has been written, there is a discussion of the case typically involving five to ten participants who are also students and writers of their own cases.

The first stage, creating an outline, consists of answering the following questions:

- **What is the organization?** It can be an organization the student has worked for in the past or is working in currently. If they haven't worked in an organization, then students can choose an organization from a list or one they have an interest in working in. It is likely that this option will require mainly secondary research on the students' part. In the cases chosen for this book, the students used organizations with which they had first-hand experience.
- **What is the problem or situation you want to analyze?** Students write a one- or two-sentence description of why they are interested in the problem and how they intend to use it for a case study.
- **What topic or topics from class does the proposed case study fall under?** The linkage of the case with topics from class begins the process, at the most rudimentary level, of applying course concepts to workplace experience. In all of the case studies, there was a main topic that the case emphasized and one or two secondary topics that the case also dealt with.

The next stage involves writing the case prospectus. This phase of the process entails fleshing out the earlier outline by the following steps:

- Briefly describe the organization on which the case will be based. A lot of this information can be found by answering the questions: What is the setting? Where, when, why did the events happen?
- Identify the key actors in the case: include the names of positions or departments as opposed to individuals. Use false names to conceal identities of actual persons.
- Provide a brief description or abstract of the case story or content including the problem/issues/opportunities and the possible actions/outcomes.
- Describe how the background research for the case will be conducted and how primary source information from the organization will be collected.
- Describe the teaching purpose of the case or how it could be used in a class similar to this one.

The third stage is conducting research for the case. This phase typically includes research using public information as well as information from personal records, published sources, and the official website. The research also includes data collected from interviews or student observations while at the organization. Once these stages have been accomplished, the student is ready to write the case.

In writing the case, the student answer the following questions:

- Is a decision maker who must act, choose, or make decisions clearly identified?
- What is the actor's job/role/position? Why must the actor take action? What kind of action, if any, must be taken?
- Is the time frame or chronology of the case clear?
- Is it important to know where important events occur? Are places/locations clearly identified?
- Can the key problems, issues, or difficulties that the decision maker must or should confront be identified?
- Is the case organized according to a logical, easy to understand outline? Are there subheads, numbered points, transitions, clear and well-labeled tables, well-organized appendices, well-reproduced charts and graphics?
- Is the case interesting and challenging? Does the case introduction arouse interest or curiosity?
- Will case readers be able to see themselves in the decision maker's role or in other roles? Are readers likely to have different opinions as to appropriate action? Will they sympathize or identify with the actor's problems? Can a relevant range of alternative courses of action be identified using information in the case?

Once the case has been written, there should be three to five questions at the end for readers to discuss. The author should be prepared to lead a small group discussion of the case. At the beginning of the discussion, the case writer is required to make a brief presentation based on the case focusing on the major elements identified in the list of questions above

When the professors graded the presentations, the following elements of the case were considered: content, case questions, data collection/research, reference page, grammar and organization, and class discussion. A sample grading rubric can be viewed in the Appendix.

ORGANIZATION OF THE BOOK

The fourteen case studies are organized around several main themes or topics of public administration, including political context of public administration, bureaucracy and organizational structure, organizational culture, leadership, human relations administration, budgeting, ethics, and decision making. These main themes have been selected because they occur in nearly every standard textbook. Furthermore, they are topics that every student in an introductory class should become familiar with, at least at some basic level. Most cases contain one or two secondary themes in addition to the main theme. As pointed out earlier, however, as instructors we ultimately had little control over the initial case idea. By using the method of requiring drafts of the different sections, we were able to help shape the form of the final product.

References

Choy, S. (2002). *Nontraditional undergraduates* (NCES, 2002–12). U.S. Department of Education: National Center for Educational Statistics. Washington, DC: U.S. Government Printing Office. http://nces.ed.gov/pubs2002/2002012.pdf, p. 3.

Electronic Hallway website. Accessed November 2009. https://hallway.org/index.php?PHPSESSID=koh6atsnhvbhnnhsuklodo25b1

Holzer, M., Redding-Raines, A., & Yu, W. (undated). *Research and information resources for public administration*. United Nations Public Administration Network and American Society for Public Administration. unpan1.un.org/intradoc/groups/public/documents/aspa/unpan020144.pdf

Knowles, M. S. (1988). *The modern practice of adult education: From pedagogy to andragogy* (rev. ed.). New York: Cambridge Book Co.

Loutzenhiser, K. K., & Orman, R. G. (2005, October). *What happens when you cross public administration with school serving adults?* Panel presentation at the annual meeting of the National Association of Schools of Public Affairs and Administration, Washington, D.C.

Lynn, L. E. (1999). *Teaching and learning with cases*. Washington, DC: CQ Press.

Merriam, S. B., & Caffarella, R. S. (1999). *Learning in adulthood*. San Francisco: Jossey Bass.

Pitts, D. W., & Wise, L. R. (2004). Diversity of professional schools: A case study of public affairs and law. *Journal of Public Affairs Education, 10*(2), 125–142.

Reid, M., & Miller, W. (1997). Bridging theory and administrative practice: The role of a capstone course in P.A. programs. *International Journal of Public Administration. 20*(10), 1769–1790.

Rice, M. F. (2004). Organizational culture, social equity, and diversity: Teaching public administration education in the postmodern era. *Journal of Public Affairs Education, 10*(2), 143–154.

Selden, S. C., & Selden, F. (2001). Rethinking diversity in public organizations for the 21st century: Moving toward a multicultural model. *Administration and Society, 33*(3), 303–329.

Soni, V. (2000). A twenty-first century reception for diversity in the public sector: A case study. *Public Administration Review, 60*(5), 395–408.

U.S. Department of Education, NCES. (2002). *Digest of education statistics 2000* (NCES 2002–130). Washington, DC: U.S. Government Printing Office.

White, S. (2004). Multicultural MPA curriculum: Are we preparing culturally competent public administrators? *Journal of Public Affairs Education, 10*(2), 111–123.

APPENDIX

CASE STUDY ASSIGNMENT FOR STUDENTS*

Description: The current assignment will give you an opportunity to write a case study for the class and, possibly, for publication in a textbook. The case should be based on a real situation in an organization, but some details may need to be fabricated in order for the case to fit with this course. The cases will be graded by the instructor and used in class by your fellow students. Some cases may be selected for future publication in a textbook of public administration cases. You will be contacted by the book editors with further details if your case is selected.

Objectives:

- To develop effective problem-solving and critical thinking skills as applicable to academic and professional contexts
- To enhance and demonstrate aptitude for scientific inquiry
- To reinforce the application of course concepts to organizational situations
- To allow students to take responsibility for learning and share with peers in the classroom

Steps:

1. Develop a Case Prospectus
   - The prospectus is an outline of the case that should include the following:
     1. What will be the main topic of the case? The topic should be applicable to the course.
     2. Briefly describe the organization on which the case will be based.
     3. Describe the setting: where, when, why.
     4. Who will be included in the case? Include the position or department names as opposed to individuals.
     5. Provide a brief description of the case story or content including the problem/issues/opportunities and the actions/outcomes.
     6. How will you conduct the background research for the case and collect primary source information from the organization?
     7. Describe the teaching purpose of the case or how it could be used in a class similar to this one.
2. Conduct Research for the Case
   - Your research may include public information as well as information from the company archives, published sources, and its website.
   - Your research should include data collected from interviews or questionnaires at the organization.
3. Write the Case
   - See sample case for an example of the case structure and content.
   - The case should consist of approximately ten pages and written in APA style with appropriate citation of resources.

---

* The assignment is adapted from the Electronic Hallway's "Welcome to the Case Method" PDF document located at https://hallway.org/cases/display_case.php?case_ID=welc.

- There should be three to five questions at the end of the case for readers to discuss. (There may not be right or wrong answers to the questions.)
- The case should answer the following questions:
  - Is a decision maker who must act, choose, or make decisions clearly identified?
  - What is the actor's job/role/position? Why must the actor take action? What kind of action must be taken?
  - Is the time frame or chronology of the case clear?
  - Is it important to know where important events occur? Are places/locations clearly identified?
  - Can the key problems, issues, or difficulties that the decision maker must or should confront be identified?
  - Is the case organized according to a logical, easy-to-understand outline? Are there subheads, numbered points, transitions, clear and well-labeled tables, well-organized appendices, well-reproduced charts and graphics?
  - Is the case interesting and challenging? Does the case introduction arouse interest or curiosity?
  - Will case readers be able to see themselves in the decision maker's role or in other roles? Are readers likely to have different opinions as to appropriate action? Will they sympathize or identify with the actor's problems? Can a relevant range of alternative courses of action be identified using information in the case?
4. Case Discussion
   - Cases will be discussed and utilized in class.

Grading Rubric

| Criteria | Performance Indicators | | |
	Needs Improvement	Meets Expectations	Exceptional
Content	Poorly developed case that answers less than 50% of the required questions	Adequate case that answers 50–75% of the required information	Case integrates resources to thoroughly answer all of the required case questions
Case Questions	Does not provide questions and/or responses, or poorly written question and or responses	Provides adequate questions and suggested responses that demonstrate some course application and critical thinking	Provides 3–5 well-written questions that are applicable to case and course; questions and responses demonstrate strong critical thinking

(continued)

Grading Rubric Continued

Criteria	Performance Indicators		
	Needs Improvement	**Meets Expectations**	**Exceptional**
Data Collection/ Research	Poor background research with few to no citations; does not use a questionnaire, structured observation, or structured interview to collect data	Adequate data collection using public sources and databases; cites research	Thoroughly collected data using public sources and databases as well as a questionnaire, structured observation, OR structured interview; accurately cites results in body of case
Application of Concepts	Lack of or improper application of course concepts	Adequately applies and integrates some course concepts within the case	Accurately uses direct application of course concepts throughout the case, demonstrating critical and analytical skills; integrates concepts with organizational information
Reference Page	No reference page or multiple mistakes in referencing sources	References sources with minimal mistakes	Accurately references all sources used in the body of the case; uses correct format on reference page
Grammar and Organization	Poorly organized and written case with numerous errors	Well-written case with minimal errors	Well-written case; free of errors in grammar, punctuation, word choice, spelling and format; paragraphs are organized well
Case Discussion	Poor preparation for discussion; minimal participation or contributions lack depth and understanding	Adequately prepared; makes contributions to discussion; poses questions	Well prepared for discussion; makes meaningful and articulate contributions; poses insightful questions to peers

1

THE STOUGHTON CITY BUDGET

Robert A. Cropf,
Jennifer M. Giancola, and
Ann Robertson

OVERVIEW

Abstract

Each year, local elected officials must exercise leadership concerning the allocation of fiscal resources. In this case, the council must decide whether to support or reject the revised budget recommendation, leaving the mayor with the deciding vote. This case study highlights the organizational and political decision-making processes that are involved in weighing the pros and cons of various budgetary options within the context of a local municipality's budget revision and approval process.

Main Topics

Financial management, Bureaucracy and structure

Secondary Topics

Leadership, Strategic management

Teaching Purpose

To examine the complexities involved in the financial planning process in the context of local government politics.

The Organization

The municipality of Stoughton, which includes a four-person city council and a mayor.

Main Characters

- Janice Miller, Mayor
- John Sellers, City Manager
- Pete Smith, Sheila McCullough, Elizabeth Banning, and Tom Richardson: City Council

BACKGROUND

Stoughton is a community of approximately 4,700 people located in a mid-western state. Founded in 1929, the community is a mid-ring suburb for the state's largest city and includes its own shopping district. Most of the housing is ranch style, built after World War II to house returning servicemen and their families. The business and shopping district is along a very busy four-lane road that bisects the community. Along this large street are several strip malls with smaller commercial buildings, many of which are reaching the end of their productive lives.

The community is racially diverse with mostly Caucasian households but with a relatively large proportion of African Americans and a small percentage of other races. The median income last year was $47,900 with 4.5 percent of the population living below the poverty level. The city's income level is close to the average for the region.

Stoughton provides its citizens with a wide range of public services. The local police and fire departments provide the community with public safety. A Park and Recreation Department maintains the city parks and coordinates community activities such as youth programs and a community day care service. The Public Works Department maintains the city facilities and roads. The Housing Department does occupancy inspections and handles building permits and construction inspections. The court hears cases, assesses fines, and issues warrants in support of the work done by the police and fire departments and the building inspectors.

THE CITY'S ADMINISTRATION

The city has a mayor/council form of government with four council members representing individual districts, also termed wards, and a city manager. The city's administration is organized with a city manager as its head. Janice Miller, a native of Stoughton, is the mayor. She is a social conservative with liberal fiscal tendencies. Her family has long been active in the business and political communities. Janice has been mayor for three years and ran her campaign on a "get it right financially" platform.

Ward 1 Councilman, Pete Smith, owns a small business in Stoughton. He is a self-described libertarian who wants as little governmental interference as possible and thinks government functions should be done as efficiently as possible. He supports cutting services that are not critical to the community's safety to meet budget constraints.

Ward 2 Councilwoman, Sheila McCullough, ideologically similar to Mayor Miller, is a native of the community and has been on the council for twenty years. She is also a retired schoolteacher. The previous mayor lied to Ms. McCullough, which has made her timid about making any major changes to city operations. She fears not getting enough or correct information from staff members, because the previous mayor controlled them and had them misrepresent information presented to the council.

Ward 3 Councilwoman, Elizabeth Banning, is a working-class resident who is very concerned with how decisions impact the "average" resident and the poor. She is a stay-at-home mother.

Ward 4 Councilman, Tom Richardson, is a young developer/real estate agent who is fiscally conservative. He brings a business perspective to the council as well as information on options for increasing revenue through development.

City Manager John Sellers has a Master's in Public Administration and ten years of experience working in distressed/disadvantaged communities. He has also worked on political campaigns and for the state attorney general's office combating consumer fraud. He is a self-described generalist who works with little staff support and few options for delegating tasks.

THE CITY'S FINANCES

Stoughton's revenue stream has been flat to declining over the past decade. The operating expenses, however, have increased by 4 to 6 percent per year for the past five years. The operating deficit began to erode Stoughton's cash reserves five years ago. The remainder of the cash reserve was used to purchase five buildings to be used as a new location for a city hall as well as three additional properties that were to be part of a redevelopment project.

Shortly after the cash reserves were depleted, the illegal activities of the previous mayor, Lance Nosworthy, were discovered. Nosworthy had staff withhold information from city council members so that new retirement contracts and expensive purchases could be made despite the fact that funds were not available to support the actions. Nosworthy, meanwhile, received kickbacks on the retirement contract and was subsequently impeached and arrested. The council was left to put the city's finances back on track. The first order of business was to secure a loan for $500,000 to cover expenses for which there was no current revenue. Stoughton was able to secure the loan using the property purchased for the new city hall site.

To address the operating shortfall, the city's budget was slashed 15 percent for the current year. The cuts meant several open staff positions went unfilled. To save funds, the city filled the open positions of police and fire chief by promoting from within the departments. This means the chiefs have less leadership experience, but their salaries were affordable within the constrained city budget. In addition, several city staff members were discharged for cause. The firings arose from the incompetence of the previous city manager and human resources director, which resulted from their collaborations with the impeached mayor.

The local newspaper, *The Clarion*, has naturally taken a great interest in the unraveling of the city's finances, and its increased coverage has led to the formation of Stoughton Citizens for Fiscal Reform, led by a prominent local banker. As a result of *The Clarion*'s and the reform group's efforts, the local citizenry is riled up. Attendance at city council meetings is greater than at any other time in the recent past. It is not unusual for the mayor and council members to have their words drowned out in the ensuing din of council meetings.

REDEVELOPMENT PLANS

The city initially took action five years ago to address declining revenues by looking for new revenue opportunities. A plan to redevelop a portion of the business district was put forward by a regional developer. This project would have replaced a small, aging strip mall and twelve homes with a single big-box retailer. However, there was significant opposition from the community because of one of the retailers in question and the plan was rejected by a divided city council.

The city council then decided to pursue a more aggressive development plan. It would be larger in scale, which would allow it to make money for a developer without putting a suburban big-box retailer on Stoughton's main shopping street. "We want a main street that retains the small business character of the community while still providing jobs for residents and sales tax revenue for the city," commented Mayor Miller. This more aggressive plan included development on both the north and south sides of the street and the displacement of forty homes.

In pursuit of this plan, the city issued a Request for Proposals (RFP). After receiving several responses, a developer was chosen. The new project would be done in two phases over five years. City support of the project would include use of eminent domain to acquire property if necessary and providing Tax Increment Financing (TIF) for construction. The city entered into a development agreement with STL Development Corporation and things were set to go. However, six months into the project, STL Development Corp. decided to back out. Changes in the regional economy had made the company nervous that the project might not make a profit. A second RFP was floated by the city. A second developer seemed interested but walked away before signing a development agreement because it believed that the city's financial support was not sufficient to cover the significant risk involved in the project. Finally, an interested developer was found who was willing to take on the project. A new development agreement was signed with Foster Development Inc., and the project was again moving forward. The local newspaper and the Stoughton Citizens for Fiscal Reform also expressed support for the new project. The city council was relieved but still concerned about the project being completed so it could start generating revenue.

THE BUDGET FORECAST

Each winter, the city staff develops a budget for the next fiscal year. The process begins with City Manager John Sellers. Sellers consults with the department heads and the city's finance officer and presents a budget to the city council that includes revenue projections, operating expenses, and capital expenses. The city council then debates, modifies if necessary, and passes a budget in March that takes effect April 1 of the subsequent year.

This year, John Sellers realized that the financial issues the city faced would have long-term impacts. Therefore, instead of the standard one-year budget, Sellers created a five-year budget forecast for planning purposes. This forecast was prepared in a similar fashion to the standard budget. Department heads prepared capital and new expense requests (see Table 1). Each request required a specific description of what was being requested, a cost projection, and in which year the need would arise. Requests included items such as new job positions, new computers, and new capital equipment. The finance officer provided the revenue projections and an estimate of normal operating expense increases.

The projections (see Table 2) are fairly conservative with revenues growing at 2 percent per year and expenses growing at 4 percent per year. Revenues have not been consistently growing, so there is a risk in forecasting a 2 percent growth rate rather than a flat forecast. On the expense side, basic inflation plus increases in health care and staff salaries may not be covered by the 4 percent increase forecast. The city has been running lean on money and this forecast will not change that.

The funding requests from each department clearly show their priorities as well as the fact that they understand the budget "game." Departments have asked for necessary items and a few "extras," knowing that the city council will not fund all the requests. Departments are hoping the extras are cut and not the more basic items.

The budget shows a number of years during which the city is running in deficit. Considering there is currently no cash reserve, this cannot happen. The state requires cities to have a balanced budget, and this budget clearly is

TABLE 1	**Department Head Budget Requests**		
Police	3 new vehicles	$75,000	2 in Year 3 1 in Year 4
	SUV command vehicle	$25,000	Year 3
	4 radar and computer mobile ticketing computers	$15,000	Year 1
Public Works	2-Ton dump truck with plow and spreader	$85,000	Year 1
	Backhoe 4 × 4 with extender	$90,000	Year 2
	Wood Chipper	$35,000	Year 3
	Pick-up truck	$45,000	Year 4

TABLE 2　Five-Year Forecast Budget

	Current Year	Budget Projection				
		Year 1	Year 2	Year 3	Year 4	Year 5
Normal Ongoing Activity						
Revenue						
Operating	$3,652,918	$3,026,850	$3,087,387	$3,149,135	$3,212,118	$3,276,360
Capital Improvements		$698,150	$712,113	$726,355	$740,882	$755,700
Operating Expenses						
Administration	$716,782	$608,300	$632,632	$657,937	$684,255	$711,625
Court	$145,969	$153,550	$158,132	$164,457	$171,063	$177,877
Fire	$770,479	$690,600	$704,122	$732,286	$761,578	$792,041
Housing	$71,100	$55,850	$57,626	$59,931	$62,329	$64,822
Park & Recreation	$169,398	$146,300	$152,152	$158,238	$164,568	$171,150
Police	$1,064,598	$924,950	$961,948	$1,000,426	$1,040,443	$1,082,061
Public Works	$730,204	$593,400	$502,944	$523,062	$543,984	$565,744
Total	$3,668,530	$3,172,950	$3,169,556	$3,296,337	$3,428,220	$3,565,320
Percentage Change	7.07%	1–3.51%	−0.11%	4.00%	4.00%	4.00%
Net Operating		($146,100)	($82,169)	($147,202)	($216,102)	($288,960)
Capital Expenses						
Road Project Match						$368,884
Net Capital		$698,150	$712,113	$726,355	$740,882	$386,816
Net Ongoing Activity	($15,612)	$552,050	$629,944	$579,153	$524,780	$97,856
One-Time Activities						
Revenues	$299,266					
Development Phase 1			$5,000	$226,000	$299,000	$311,000
Development Phase 2					$192,137	$197,901
Expenses						
Administration		$50,000				
Fire	$107,300		$6,000	$6,000	$6,000	$6,000
Police	$186,096		$16,049	$15,000		
Public Works	$45,555		$85,000	$90,000	$35,000	$45,000
Court			$4,500	$1,500	$1,500	$1,600
Park and Recreation			$12,000	$35,000	$40,000	$20,000
Street Bond (5MM, 20yr)			$408,345	$518,345	$518,340	$517,705
Police Car			$50,000		$25,000	$50,000
Fire House (mortgage)				$77,879	$77,879	$77,879
Fire Truck (loan)				$65,860	$65,860	$65,860
City Hall (mortgage)			$79,836	$79,836	$79,836	$79,836
Net One Time Activities	($39,685)	($50,000)	($656,730)	($663,420)	($358,278)	($354,979)
Bottom Line Net	($55,297)	$502,050	($26,786)	($84,267)	$166,503	($257,123)

not in balance. Therefore, the years in the red serve as a warning to the council that something will have to be done to prevent a deficit from occurring.

The budget was then presented to the council. During the meeting with department heads, council members were particularly concerned with the large number of expensive items on the capital lists. Each department presented the council with a list of action items. The lists of items, for example, were clarified to include priority ratings as follows:

Public Works

- 2-Ton Dump Truck
- Backhoe
- Pick-up Truck
- Wood Chipper

Park and Recreation

- Comprehensive Plan—critical for Community Development Block Grant funds
- New roof on office building
- Road assessment study
- New copier and computer
- Park shelter
- Office renovations
- Develop existing property into park area

The council inquired as to whether the Public Works Department could enter into leasing agreements with nearby municipalities that would allow them to "borrow" trucks and other heavy equipment. Council members also questioned whether a new park shelter and office renovations were necessary when the city was in a belt-tightening mode.

Specific questions were also asked about why the police department needs so many vehicles. There are only four officers on duty at any time and the chief needs a vehicle at all times. The new vehicles requested would put the department at nine vehicles. Councilman Smith commented that a more reasonable number would be six so each on-duty officer and the chief has a vehicle and there is one spare for when a vehicle is being repaired. Councilwoman McCullough disagreed, saying that there have been emergencies where all cars were used and keeping police services a priority will "maintain community confidence."

The council had a long discussion about the need for a fire station. Everyone was in agreement that the fire station cannot stay where it is for long. The rented building is not designed for permanent use and the site is part of Phase 2 of the redevelopment plan, which is a critical piece of the city's future revenues. However, the council was split on what should be done. Council members Richardson and Smith expressed that the department is not meeting the needs of the community because it is too small. They proposed merging the department with another community nearby to get better service and save on capital expenses for new equipment. A building may still need to be constructed, but only after an agreement is reached with an adjoining community so that the coverage issue can be addressed. Council members McCullough and Banning disagreed.

Councilwoman McCullough suggested that having a fire department that is accountable directly to the city manager and mayor is critical to meeting citizens' desires for prompt and appropriate service. Councilwoman Banning was concerned that a merger could leave firefighters who have been on the force for a short time out of a job. This would impact two firefighters with young families who live in the community.

At the next meeting, City Manager Sellers presented the full budget forecast. Sellers's presentation included materials from other communities to show comparative expenses and information on the overall economy. City Manager Sellers had some structural recommendations for the budget. The city must get operating expenses down to within the revenue stream (currently the city spends capital revenues on operations). This will require additional department reductions as well as splitting the public works expenses between capital maintenance (a capital expense) and regular operations. Also, the city needs to work toward having a 30 percent cash reserve. This will cushion operations for cash flow since revenue is unevenly received as well as provide funds in case of emergencies.

City Manager Sellers's other budget recommendations included contracting out Public Works and Park and Recreation departments to adjoining communities within the next year. Sellers has already broached the topic with two communities and they are willing to discuss it. This would save operating expenses and split capital expenses for large items with another community. In addition, Sellers recommended contracting out fire services delivery to a nearby municipality. This change will take longer to negotiate and will likely generate more public opposition. He conveyed that it is important because the fire department is expensive and small and cannot meet the expanding needs in the community for ambulance service because it lacks training and equipment. These deficits cannot be addressed within the current finance situation.

Finally, Sellers recommended that the land purchased for a new city hall be converted to private ownership. The revenue would be sufficient to pay back the $500,000 in debt as well as leave some funds for use as a cash reserve. City hall is currently being run out of a retail storefront. It is not fancy, but it is working. Sellers suggested that within the next year, the city could move administrative operations to the Park and Recreation building since that department would be consolidated with an adjoining city that has additional office space. This would save the city from paying rent and would keep operations going. This would not be the long-term solution, but it would allow the city to wait until its fiscal situation improves with the opening of the new development project. At that time, the city can make a decision about building a city hall. This will leave the court, fire, and police operations in rented facilities, but it has been working for the past year and can continue for a while longer.

TIME FOR A VOTE

Council members Richardson and Smith are fully in support of City Manager Sellers recommendations. They think the dire fiscal circumstances warrant this change in city operations to meet the long-term needs of citizens. Councilwoman McCullough thinks this plan is drastic and decides to vote against it unless additional information regarding options is gained from outside sources to verify what staff is recommending. Councilwoman Banning is against it because firefighters, Public Works employees, and Park and Recreation Department employees could lose their jobs.

The Clarion and the Citizens for Fiscal Reform whole heartedly support the city manager's recommendations, in particular the aggressive use of contracting out.

Mayor Miller calls the vote because this is the last council meeting before the end of the fiscal year. A no vote on the budget will force staff to scramble to revise the budget and present it again. Roll call is taken:

Councilwoman Banning:	No
Councilwoman McCullough:	No
Councilman Richardson:	Yes
Councilman Smith:	Yes

The tie vote means Mayor Miller must cast her vote. The mayor hesitates but in the end she knows that she must exercise the leadership the city looks to her to provide.

Discussion Questions

1. Which requested capital expenses from the lists would you cut and why?
2. Would you contract services out to another community? How would you convince the council to support a change that might affect constituents negatively?
3. Would you vote to raise taxes? Explain.
4. Would you build a new city hall or continue to use existing facilities? If so, how would you raise the money to pay for it?
5. If you were Mayor Miller how would you vote? Explain.

2 | SOCIAL SECURITY ADMINISTRATION CASE

Robert A. Cropf,
Jennifer M. Giancola, and
Christine Latinette

OVERVIEW

Abstract

As organizations grow to meet increasing demands for services, old systems and processes can start to break down, resulting in inefficiencies that give rise to increasing frustration on the part of employees and service recipients. Under these circumstances, achieving a fair review process for citizens can be a trying affair for everyone concerned. This case focuses on both the individual and organizational dilemmas raised in attempting to provide a fair and transparent process for receiving benefits.

Main Topics

Bureaucracy and structure, Human resources administration

Secondary Topics

Intergovernmental affairs, Ethics

Teaching Purpose

To examine the difficulties encountered while trying to balance the demands of both job and citizen in terms of responsibility, accountability, and equity; and to raise issues concerning the treatment of disabled citizens by public agencies.

The Organization

The U.S. Social Security Administration is an independent agency of the United States that administers Social Security, a social insurance program consisting of retirement, disability, and survivors' benefits.

Main Characters

- Vince Rogov, a veteran seeking disability benefits
- Mike Lawrence, Disability Advocate

BACKGROUND

The Social Security Administration (SSA), the organization in question, has the characteristics of both a social welfare organization and a typical large federal agency. Social welfare organizations have a unique set of factors that determines their structure and culture. These organizations are designed to serve people, many of whom often have great needs. Complicating this, however, is the fact that—typically—federal agencies, due to their size and scope, are top-down bureaucracies. For example, a single printed policy manual for SSA employees is composed of fifty separate three-inch binders. In order to try to compensate for its bureaucratic structure and to respond to the changing roles of the agency, SSA emphasizes a more flexible response and more employee involvement.

Commissioner of Social Security JoAnn Barnhart described the goals of the agency as service, stewardship, solvency, and staff. Decreasing budgets and a smaller workforce, at the same time that application caseloads are increasing, can lead to conflicts in pursuing all of these goals. In light of these challenges, SSA workers must strive to achieve an ambitious agenda— nothing less than meeting the social security needs and expectations of the American people. These workers are required to exhibit the values of respect, responsiveness, and reliability in accomplishing this daunting task. Clearly, these employees are faced with a challenge.

At the same time, they are committed employees, who are dedicated to their jobs, as exemplified by the fact that the agency was ranked seventh by its workers in the Best Places to Work in Federal Government Survey. SSA workers also have a great deal of respect for one another, ranking the agency third in the same survey in team orientation. They find their work meaningful because it eventually touches the lives of every American citizen. The same survey identified some serious problems, however. One problem is leadership. Since the agency's executives are political appointees, who turn over with every new presidential administration, the change at the top can lead to serious disruptions in the agency. As a result, SSA workers give the agency low scores for effective leadership.

Disability Insurance (DI) is one of the three major programs administered by SSA, along with Old Age and Survivor Insurance (OASI) and Supplemental Security Income (SSI). The work of administering disability benefit claims has risen dramatically in recent years. During the five-year period from 2000 to 2005, applications for disability insurance increased 60 percent to more than two million. Billions of dollars are now paid in disability benefits. This explosive growth has caused a significant backlog of cases, which can extend for months or even years, from the initial application. In his testimony to Congress in February 2007, Sylvester Schieber, chair of the Social Security Advisory Board, highlighted many issues that contribute to this flood of cases. Perhaps most important are the dual factors of technology and insufficient resources. Thus, while commending the recent improvement in technology and electronic application and review, he reiterated a call for funding appropriate to the growing list of duties this agency must deliver.

THE DISABILITY BENEFITS PROCESS

The process of applying for disability benefits can be long and arduous. Each state's Disability Determination Service (DDS) is charged with conducting the initial review and referral. The standards for determination vary from state to state. This lack of uniformity presents some significant problems for both agency employees and citizens. Obtaining disability benefits is subject to certain basic qualification requirements. First, the worker must have an established work history with a minimum number of employment periods based on age. Second, the length of the disability itself must be expected to last a minimum of twelve months. In some states, the DDS erroneously referred pregnant workers for Social Security Disability, despite the fact that the length of pregnancy would not meet the minimum time required. These flawed referrals, however, may be an attempt by a state to pass along its funding burden to the federal government. Third, and perhaps most important, the disability must be so severe as to eliminate employment in any occupation. Disability is not allowed if a worker can engage in any activity that can generate another source of income. For example, an airline pilot may no longer be able to fly a plane, but he/she may be able to obtain employment as a flight teacher. If this is the case, the ex-pilot does not meet the qualification for disability benefit approval.

After meeting the initial criteria, an applicant is then referred to the federal Social Security Administration. Here the input from field workers becomes crucial. Observational data and any documentation of disability must accompany the application. The majority of SSA workers are conscientious in assisting in the completion of an application. They are unbiased in their assessment of the situation and attempt to present a fair and accurate statement of the disability. In certain cases, a physician's input is required as well. These observations may influence the decision to allow or deny benefits. Mental illness presents perhaps the most challenging disability decision. Whereas physical disability may be temporary and treatable, in psychiatric cases, the expectation of improvement may be less certain. Moreover, the system is not exempt from fraud. In some cases, unscrupulous citizens have been known to collect undeserved benefits. Here the caseworker must balance the citizens' service needs against other agency goals, including stewardship and fiscal responsibility.

An issue with the process becomes apparent after the initial application for benefits. Until recently, the only time review of decisions was allowed was after benefits were awarded. There was virtually no review for cases that resulted in denial of benefits. Given the constrained budget and political pressures, denial was therefore quite common for initial decisions, with the exception of the most obvious and compelling cases. Only recently has some review of the denial of benefits become a part of the decision-making process and even then on a sporadic basis.

When denial occurs, it is the function of the caseworker to inform the applicant. Not surprisingly, the denial is met with emotions such as anger, sorrow, frustration, confusion, and often feelings of being insulted. Caseworkers attempt to diffuse the denial message by informing the applicant of his/her right to appeal and providing educational material on the appeals process. However, the multistep appeals process is exhausting and frequently can take years for claims to be decided. In a few instances, appeals have even reached the U.S. Supreme Court. Unfortunately, applicants have sometimes died waiting for their claim to be decided.

THE CLIENT ADVOCACY COMMUNITY

An advocacy community has gradually evolved in response to the growing backlog of disability cases. The appeals process requires an in-depth knowledge of legal procedure, medical expertise, and an encyclopedic understanding of the rules and regulations governing the Social Security system. The average disabled worker does not possess the ability or skills to navigate this path by himself/herself. Qualified advocates are therefore needed to fill this role. Given their expertise and their ability to successfully navigate what is a veritable maze, these advocates often demand fees for their services.

Advocates connect with clients through a variety of means, including walk-ins, phone-ins, and referrals. Their fee is contingent on the award of retroactive benefits to an applicant. Typically, the fee equals 25 percent of the dollar value of an award. Moreover, because the backlog for a case may exceed three years, a retroactive judgment can be significant. Advocates are not motivated by the fees alone, however; many have a background in social service and are seeking to achieve a fair outcome for their clients.

A symbiotic relationship has come into being between advocates and private long-term disability insurance coverage providers. Typically, the insurer is already paying benefits to the disabled worker. Because insurance coverage is integrated with Social Security disability payments, there is motivation for the insurer to seek federal benefits to offset or replace the private insurance benefits. If the advocate helps the client obtain a Social Security disability payment, the insurer may be able to reduce or eliminate the private coverage expense. As a result, insurers do a thorough job of documenting the cause of disability for everyone involved. In many cases, these referrals are then ready for an advocate.

At the same time, advocates are experts in the appeals and application processes. They make sure that all the paperwork required by the Social Security Administration is completed to the letter. As the demands of the agency increase, SSA workers have come to have a true appreciation for the role advocates play in expediting many aspects of application or appeal. A truly collaborative relationship often results between agency workers and advocates.

VINCE'S CASE

When Vince Rogov initially entered Mike Lawrence's office, both Vince and his case seemed reasonable enough. Vince had multiple medical problems, including hypertension, a history of cardiac arrest, and back problems. Furthermore, his medical issues were well documented by physicians at the Veteran's Administration (VA) hospital. Vince, however, mentioned to Mike some psychiatric problems as well, which he brushed off as minor. Despite multiple medical and psychiatric issues, Vince had been denied disability benefits by SSA several times. After an introductory interview, Mike decided to take Vince's appeals case.

As his research progressed, Mike unearthed more details of Vince's disabilities. It was during Vince's military service in Iraq that his mental illness began to manifest. He served as a private first class from March 2003 to May 2004. It was during this time that Vince first reported having great difficulty maintaining or engaging in interpersonal relationships. His family and friends said Vince had irreparably severed ties with them. His recent history included several violent episodes and encounters with the military police. He had already accumulated a significant police record at the time of the interview, including numerous weapons charges. After his return from Iraq, Vince's life and grip on reality quickly unraveled. He reported not remembering where he spent the night on many occasions and began having hallucinations.

Mike believed that an appeal with competent legal representation would favorably resolve the impasse. At the most recent meeting, he observed Vince's growing agitation, as he attempted to manage Vince's scheduling expectations. After the advocate's appeals filing, as is standard procedure, the administrative law judge (ALJ) requested that Mike arrange to represent Vince at a hearing of the evidence and testimony. The ALJ also wished to observe Vince. Mike contacted Vince to confirm the appointment. It was at this time that Vince's personality took a violent turn. Vince told Mike that he would be happy to appear. He wanted to get together with all the parties because he was going to shoot everyone: the field worker, Mike, the ALJ, and himself. Mike was understandably shaken and concerned. Clearly, Vince believed that he had nothing to lose by his outburst.

The next day, however, Vince called Mike and apologized profusely. He said he had been drinking and did not mean a word he said to Mike the day before. Vince promised that he would never say or do anything that would cause harm to anyone else. The outburst was, in fact, due to the unbearable amount of stress the case had been putting him through. Mike, however, was understandably skeptical. Although Vince sounded reasonable on the phone, Mike considered Vince's recent psychological history and could not definitively say that Vince had not been serious in his intention to harm. It was a few minutes before he was scheduled to meet with the ALJ. As he walked down the long corridor to the judge's chambers, Mike pondered the situation.

Discussion Questions

1. Who are the stakeholders? What internal and external stakeholder conflicts do you see?
2. What actions would you recommend for the ALJ?
3. What is the significance of the federal government's role in the case? The state government's role? Explain.
4. What influence do you think Vince's threat presents in decision making? Explain.
5. What are Mike's ethical obligations to Vince? To the SSA?

3 HOLY SPIRIT CHURCH BOOKKEEPER CASE

Robert A. Cropf,
Jennifer M. Giancola, and
Jessica Tietjen

OVERVIEW

Abstract

This case focuses on a church that oversees a homeless center. The center, classified as a 501 (c)(3) nonprofit organization by the federal tax code, provides free meals and shelter for the destitute. The case examines the actions of a bookkeeper for the faith-based nonprofit who decides to make up a shortfall in the operating expenses of the shelter by using a questionable method. Further, the case raises the issue of bureaucratic oversight as being important even in small organizations.

Main Topics

Decision making, Bureaucracy and structure

Secondary Topics

Ethics, Financial management

Teaching Purpose

To examine the difficulties encountered by individuals and organizations that try to balance the practical demands of organizational fiscal responsibility and transparency with the demands of professional and organizational values.

The Organization

The Holy Spirit Church is a nonprofit organization with a congregation of approximately 850 members. The Holy Spirit Haven is a 501 (c)(3) that is administered by the church but has a separate financial structure, although it is directly overseen by the church's administration.

Main Characters

- Jason Pitt, Former Director of Holy Spirit Haven
- Kevin Hitchcock, Operations Director
- Mark Hanes, Church Council's Treasurer
- Suzie Smith, Bookkeeper

BACKGROUND

This case involves a faith-based organization called the Holy Spirit Church, which is based in a major metropolitan area. Churches are a distinct type of nonprofit known as faith-based organizations. Faith-based organizations often provide social services to individuals without profit. Additionally, a faith-based nonprofit organization has its mission, values, and ethics based on a set of core religious beliefs. However, like many larger nonprofits, churches are typically bureaucratic organizations with a set hierarchy, similar to the federal government. Furthermore, the shelter operated by the church, the Holy Spirit Haven for the Homeless, has its own mission and ethical code and is under the umbrella of the larger organization.

Understanding the nature, mission, and purpose of the Holy Spirit Church is important in distinguishing it from other nonprofits. The nature of the church and shelter is clearly unlike that of typical organizations, even other nonprofits, because it derives its vitality from the religious beliefs and faith-inspired work of all the individuals within the organization. The Haven's mission statement asserts that the shelter's purpose is to help the homeless in a way that reflects the church's fundamental religious purpose. Thus, the mission makes clear that values, particularly religious faith, are essential to understanding the culture and operations of the organization and its personnel.

THE HOLY SPIRIT CHURCH

The Holy Spirit Church consists of 850 members and has an income of more than $1.2 million. To better understand the significance of this revenue, one must compare it to the national average for similar churches. If the total income of the national church organization were divided evenly among its 500 affiliates, each congregation would have an income of only $253,758. However, the Holy Spirit Church has five times that amount, which is an indication of the size and relative importance of this affiliate to the national organization. The Holy Spirit Church is easily the largest single revenue generator in the entire country.

The church has a number of paid employees, both professionals and staff. The majority of the positions have responsibilities limited to only their particular field. All of the positions within the church operate independently; each individual is assigned to cover a particular task and will ask for assistance from others when needed. The two positions that do have some degree of oversight are the director of operations and the pastor. The responsibilities of the director of operations are facility maintenance, facility schedule, staff benefits, fellowship events, outside groups, cemetery maintenance, and stewardship. The pastor's responsibilities are worship, staff support, pastoral care, and adult spiritual growth. Neither the pastor nor the director of operations has the explicit responsibility of direct oversight over the other employees of the church.

Another aspect of the organization is the church council. The council is made up of nine members of the congregation who have been elected to their position by the other parishioners. The executive committee of the council includes the president, vice president (president elect), treasurer, and secretary. The council is the board of directors of the congregation, and as such it is responsible for maintaining and protecting its property and the management of its business and fiscal affairs. Some of the council's responsibilities include the following:

- To oversee the life and activities of the congregation;
- To oversee and provide for the administration of the congregation;
- To maintain supportive relationships with the pastor and staff;
- To promote a congregational climate of peace and goodwill, and, as differences and conflicts arise, to endeavor to foster mutual understanding; and
- To be responsible for the financial and property matters of the congregation.

Clearly, the church council has the primary authority over the staff at the church. However, the council meets only once a month and consists of individuals who have other jobs and responsibilities. Although they are active members of the church, they do not have daily interaction with the church staff. According to the church charter, the council is held accountable by the congregation and by one another.

Haven for the Homeless

The Holy Spirit Church's mission statement is central to its sponsorship of the Haven for the Homeless shelter. The shelter is open all year round and is staffed largely by volunteers, most of whom are members of the church but also some who are not. In addition, the shelter is run by a director and its finances are managed by the church's accountant. The director, Lydia Daniels, is a full-time employee of the church, a recent MBA, and a longtime church member. Enrique Smith, the accountant, works part-time and provides her services to the church on a volunteer basis.

The church and the Haven, while technically separate due to the nonprofit organization status of the center, are in reality closely affiliated. The board that oversees the Haven's operations and finances consists of the church's council members and is headed by the pastor of the church. It is to this board of trustees that the shelter's director, Jason Pitt, must ultimately answer for his every action. This has never been an issue with either the Haven or the church in the past as both entities believed that the close ties between them were advantageous rather than a liability.

THE CASE OF SUZIE SMITH

Suzie Smith is thirty-two, but she has already lived a very difficult life marked by the traumatic events of her childhood. As a small child, she grew up in a broken home. Her stepfather was extremely abusive to her mother, ultimately murdering her when Suzie was only eight years old. Suzie witnessed the event, which left a permanent psychological scar. She was then taken in by her Aunt Lana's family, where she lived until she started college, all the while constantly haunted by the tragic events of her life. Suzie's nightmares would keep her up nights until they were finally controlled by medication and therapy.

Nonetheless, Suzie finally felt secure and happy in her aunt's home. Her early experiences gave her a deep understanding of and empathy toward the plight of the poor and dispossessed. In high school, she excelled in track and was elected class treasurer. On weekends and holidays, she volunteered at local homeless shelters. She graduated eighteenth out of a class of 450. Suzie received a full scholarship from the state university, where she majored in accounting. She went on to get her MBA from the same university.

Aunt Lana was very religious. Suzie, who looked up to her as if she were her true mother, accompanied her aunt to church every Sunday. Even when she moved away to college, Suzie continued her regular church attendance. After graduation, she took a job at the Holy Spirit Church, as the ministry facilitator. Two years later, she was personally asked by the pastor to become the church's bookkeeper, a full-time position with a great deal of responsibility. Her job was to keep financial records of the church, to record all receipts and pay all the bills, as well as to manage the church's finances. In this position, she had access to all the church's and the shelter's financial information and records.

During the first five years in her position, the church enjoyed tremendous growth, and the budget nearly doubled. The Haven also expanded the scope of its operations around this time. It increased its outreach efforts to the local homeless population and, as a result, experienced a nearly threefold increase in the number of individuals and families served. As a result of the tremendous growth, the church council decided that the church building could no longer accommodate the Haven and approved the construction of a brand-new facility to house just the shelter. The church council then embarked on an ambitious five-year capital program to raise money to build the shelter. In the beginning, contributions poured into the shelter construction fund. However, two years into the capital campaign, a bad economy slowed the contributions.

CRISIS IN THE SHELTER

As contributions were declining, Jason, the shelter's director, continued to ask Suzie for supplementary money. The Haven was running out of items for the shelter. At times, the Haven had to turn away people for the night because there was no more room. Making matters worse, winter was approaching so there would be an increase in the number of individuals requiring shelter. Jason and Suzie pled with the council to increase the funds available for the shelter. The council, while expressing deep sympathy for the shelter's predicament, reluctantly told them that the church's income was barely enough to meet its own budget; the Haven would, unfortunately, have to cut back on its spending. Thus, instead of money from the church, the shelter would have to make do with whatever it could raise by way of donations.

Suzie had become increasingly frustrated with this turn of events. Jason was considering resigning as the head of the Haven. There was a vacuum of leadership in the church, as the council could not find a new pastor to replace the one who left a few months before. The council, although well intentioned, was tentative in its decision making and not unified enough to provide sufficient direction to Suzie.

A crisis occurred when Jason had to take a brief leave of absence to take care of an ailing parent. In the interim, the council asked Suzie to temporarily fill the position. She was flattered that the council respected her enough to make the request, but she was also daunted by the prospect of running the shelter.

On assuming the interim directorship, the direness of the shelter's situation became painfully clear to Suzie. There was much that Jason hid from the council and, as it turned out, from her as well. Suzie, as the church's accountant, was always aware of the shelter's deficit and perilous finances, but in her new position, she began to realize the impact of the shelter's financial situation on the community. She was increasingly torn between fulfilling her obligation as the steward of the church's finances and making sure that the shelter continued to operate. Then, one day, a surprise discovery brought the issue to a head.

In going through old financial documents, Suzie discovered shares of stock that had been donated to the church a long time ago and since forgotten. Included with the stocks was an old newspaper story showing a picture of a former pastor receiving the initial gift of $10,000 worth of shares in a company just then getting started. In the years since, the little company, which makes miniature electronics components, has grown into a large, successful corporation. Suzie checked with a stockbroker friend and found out the stocks were now worth more than $1 million.

Running through Suzie's head was the thought that she could cash in the stocks and use the money to get the Haven back on its feet financially. She realized this might entail deceiving the church council, but she rationalized this deceit by thinking that worst of all would be to allow the homeless shelter to fail. Even though Suzie felt remorseful about going around the council, she also believed that the organization was not living up to its own mission by underfunding the shelter. For the next several months, Suzie took money from the church by selling off the stocks and transferring the proceeds to the shelter.

In March, the new director of operations, Kevin, discovered the transfers in going through the budget. Since no individual had the specific responsibility to oversee the bookkeeper's work with the funds of the church, the transfers had gone unnoticed for quite a while. Kevin's initial reaction was one of concern because the amount was far in excess of what the church had agreed to provide for the shelter's operations. The director thought it was time to have a serious talk with Suzie to get to the bottom of the situation.

Before doing so, however, he checked the church's accounts to see how costly Suzie's actions had been. At this point, the director decided to postpone his conversation with Suzie until he could investigate the situation more, and then, to follow the proper procedures for handling the matter as set forth in the church policy manual.

Kevin found other charges and receipts indicating that there had been multiple transfers to the Haven that had not been properly vetted by the council. Kevin and the treasurer notified the president and the executive committee of the church council because there was currently no pastor. The council held a special executive session at the church to discuss the situation. An executive session means that the records will be sealed for a designated period. At the meeting, the members of the council were shocked to learn that the trusted, well-liked Suzie could engage in such deception. All of the council members knew Suzie well and thought that they could completely trust her. After much heated discussion, the council decided that Suzie would be immediately suspended for her actions and that designated individuals would meet and talk with her before moving forward. Additionally, the treasurer had been in contact with a lawyer in order to get his advice prior to the meeting. The lawyer's advice was to first attempt to get the money back from the Haven and keep the situation quiet. The council agreed to take this course of action depending on what Suzie had to say.

Kevin and a couple other members of the church council approached Suzie and asked her to prepare a statement for the council. She was also suspended until after her appearance and more information concerning the transfers could be gathered. The council agreed to have another executive meeting, which would have Suzie's situation as its only agenda item.

At the meeting at the church, Suzie told the church council about finding the stock and subsequently selling some of it to help pay the shelter's expenses. She explained the pressure she felt as the homeless shelter had to cut back its services. After hearing Suzie, the council's main criticism was that Suzie knowingly withheld important financial information from the church and that she superseded the council's judgment with her own regarding how the money should be spent. Furthermore, she was technically in violation of several of the national church's rules regarding how church money should be spent as well as in violation of the church's ethical code. The attorney also believed that Suzie broke the law in selling church property without the approval of its governing body.

The treasurer, with the help of the new bookkeeper, had secured all of the accounts and had done a damage assessment. The approximate amount of money that should have gone to the church was $75,000. Although many of the council believed that Suzie's heart was in the right place, they thought that the decision to spend the money was not hers to make alone. The treasurer reported that the possible cause of not identifying the transfers sooner was that the bank statements had not been reconciled from December through April. Suzie had obstructed the council's access to the statements and maintained access to the church's credit cards after leaving her former position as bookkeeper. The council determined that Suzie's deceit was the source of the problem and did not make any changes to the structure of the church.

As a result of the meeting, Suzie recognizes that although her intentions were compassionate, her actions were unethical and, perhaps, illegal. Nonetheless, she is convinced that the church should spend the money on the homeless shelter. Furthermore, she does not have the money to pay back what has already been spent by the shelter. The council is unsure on how to proceed. Clearly, Suzie's actions constitute serious infractions on multiple levels. However, in the public eye, her crime likely will be viewed as one of compassion as she did not materially benefit from the sale of church-owned stock. If the church decides to pursue legal action against Suzie or otherwise harshly penalize her, it risks incurring ill will both within the church and in the outside community. Already, some homeless people from the Haven and church members have threatened to stage a protest if Suzie is punished.

Discussion Questions

1. How should the church council deal with Suzie? Explain.

2. What effect has the church's organizational structure had on the situation? In particular, what effect has it had on the overall accountability of its staff and council?

3. What should Suzie have done after she found the old stocks? Why?

4. What mechanisms could the organization put in place to guarantee transparency and prevent this type of situation from occurring in the future?

5. The case involves a faith-based nonprofit; could such a situation occur in a nonprofit that is not faith based? In a governmental agency? Would the type of organization involved make a difference in terms of what happened and outcomes? Why?

4 THE RIO ESTRECHO AUTHORITY

Robert A. Cropf,
Jennifer M. Giancola, and
Scott Crawford

OVERVIEW

Abstract

Organizations, whether in the public, nonprofit, or private sector, often must contend with the divisive issue of the perceived conflict between the institution's interests and employees' or community's interests. The Rio Estrecho Authority, a special district government, administers and regulates waterways of the Rio Estrecho basin. Recent events have required the organization to consider alternative retrenching strategies. This leads to a situation that requires an employee to make a difficult decision. The values and norms within a given organization are often subject to alternative interpretations in dynamic, high-stress environments. This case study examines the individual, administrative dilemmas raised by these issues in the context of organizational decision-making processes.

Main Topics

Bureaucracy and structure, Decision making

Secondary Topics

Political context, Intergovernmental relations

Teaching Purpose

To examine the difficulties of balancing organizational demands and both professional and individual responsibility; it also discusses issues surrounding intergovernmental and political accountability and transparent communication to employees and the community.

The Organization

The Rio Estrecho Authority (REA). The Spanish Lake Project (SLP) operates under the auspices of the REA.

Main Characters
- Thomas Fernandez, CEO of Rio Estrecho Authority
- David Winter, Southern Regional Director
- Daniel Kraves, Head Operations Officer for Spanish Lake Project
- James Blackstock, member of the special group
- Travis Cole, Dean Burke, the other members of the special group

BACKGROUND

Beginning in the 1960s, southwestern states and the metropolitan regions within those states began to experience rapid population growth that has lasted to the present day. During this time, Regional City evolved from a mid-sized, provincial town to one of the largest cities in the nation. As the city and its surrounding suburbs grew at a rapid rate, so did the need and demand for a new reservoir that could meet the water supply requirements of the area. Consequently, in 1970, the Rio Estrecho Authority (REA) in conjunction with the state government and Regional City decided to dam the Rio Estrecho and create a lake that would include parts of four nearby rural counties.

From its inception, the Spanish Lake Project (SLP) was unpopular in the two counties that stood to lose the most from its construction. Madison and San Patricio Counties would lose whole towns, cemeteries, and farmland to the advancing waters of the newly formed lake. Lacking the financial and political resources to fight against the construction of Spanish Lake, the citizens of these two counties were ultimately powerless to stop its construction. In 1974, the dam was completed and large portions of Madison and San Patricio Counties were submerged beneath its waters. From that moment on, a strong sense of enmity existed between those who administered the lake and those who were displaced by it. This animosity lasted for nearly a decade.

Upon completion of the dam, REA built a facility to house the administration of the SLP. The SLP facility initially had an adversarial relationship with the local population, resulting in the inefficient management of the lake's resources. This, however, began to change in 1982 with the hiring of Daniel Kraves as the Spanish Lake Project facility manager. Born and raised in Madison County, Kraves understood the concerns of the local population. In turn, the residents were cautiously optimistic about the hiring of "one of their own." Moreover, over time, Kraves changed how the SLP did business. He began by hiring Madison and San Patricio county residents for SLP jobs, which gradually resulted in a dominant local perspective, both culturally and politically, taking shape within the organization. Subsequently, Kraves, through the force of his personality and the goodwill engendered by a now predominantly local workforce, succeeded in persuading the surrounding communities of the viability of the lake as a financial resource. As the years passed, Daniel Krave's leadership style came to characterize the SLP's relationship with nearby communities.

Although the SLP's main purpose was to provide water for the greater Regional City area, it also became a recreational haven for many of the state's residents. Boating, fishing, and camping provided both entertainment and financial opportunities for the local population. All these were in due course licensed and taxed by REA through the auspices of the SLP. The revenue generated thereby was a boon for both the REA and the local communities. As a result both the SLP and the nearby towns grew during the decade. By the mid-1980s, the SLP had become an integral part of the community, providing either directly or indirectly employment opportunities for a large portion of the local residents. Rather than hating the REA, the residents of Madison and San Patricio Counties began to rely on income derived from the lake.

At the center of this economic upswing was the SLP. In both practical and symbolic terms, the SLP become for many locals an extension of the community. Increasing revenues from licensing and taxes resulted in the steady expansion of the SLP during those years. Staff increased from 30 in 1974 to 165 by 1985 with almost all these employment opportunities being filled by the local residents. The SLP became the single largest employer in San Patricio County and the second largest in Madison County.

Daniel Kraves received a lot of credit in the sleepy hamlets of the region for the successes of the SLP. He cultivated this acclaim and built the ethos of the SLP on the principle that, unlike its parent organization, REA, he and his employees put the local community first. Often seen shaking hands and encouraging both employees and local residents in their endeavors, Kraves's hands-on, casual approach to leadership became the *modus operandi* of the SLP. Both on a practical and a philosophical level, the SLP under Kraves's leadership began to consider itself separate and unique in comparison to the REA as a whole.

The SLP expanded as an organization well into the 1990s. Revenues from licensing, permits, and other recreational activities continued to grow, further solidifying the already close relationship the SLP had with the community. To many locals, the SLP was now an integral part of the community it served. Loyalty to one was tantamount to loyalty to the other. Therefore, when Kraves left in 1995 to become county commissioner of Madison County, the local residents were concerned that the SLP would lose its close identification with the community. Appreciating the unique situation of the SLP, REA selected for the job Kraves's handpicked successor: Ben Kraves, his son. Ben, having worked for the SLP since graduating from college, fully embraced his father's vision of the organization and understood its role in the surrounding communities.

Ben proved a very able and popular administrator, who took charge of SLP just when Spanish Lake began to experience a real estate boom. Seen as an attractive alternative to the urban and suburban settings of greater Regional City, new residential and commercial developments began to appear in earnest. This proliferation of summer homes, expansive marinas, and trendy restaurants created an entirely new revenue stream for the authority. As the lake region grew so did the SLP. Over the next decade, the SLP grew to include more than 400 full-time, part-time and seasonal employees. As the SLP increased in terms of workforce size so, too, did its economic importance to the people of Madison and San Patricio Counties.

ORGANIZATION

The state legislature created the REA as a special district government in 1955 and charged it with three major functions, which included "maintenance of a Master Plan for basin-wide development, serving as local sponsor for federal water projects and providing services authorized by the Legislature within REA's defined territory." This defined territory encompasses the seventeen counties that are in the Rio Estrecho's watershed. The authority operates a wide variety of facilities, which include wastewater treatment plants, water supply and storage projects, and recreation facilities. The REA receives no direct funding from state tax revenues and therefore must find alternative ways of financing, which include the selling of water, commercial and marina leases on water projects, and funding by cities that need water suppliers.

The structure of the organization includes a board of directors composed of twenty-four members who are appointed by the governor and approved by the state senate. These board members come from the counties that are within the jurisdiction of the REA, and it is their responsibility to decide on policy initiatives, which the REA then carries out. The main offices of the REA are the General office, which shares headquarters with the Northern Region office, and the Southern Region office.

The Southern Region office is a small facility of about thirty administrators and staff who function mainly as an administrative, information, and decision-making conduit between its subunits and the general manager, executive committee, and the board of directors of REA (see the Appendix). According to the organizational chart, the SLP reports directly to the Southern Region office; however, in practice, because of the size of the operation and the revenue it generates, it tends to function more like an autonomous unit. The SLP is structurally a reflection of its parent organization, the REA. As such, the SLP, like the REA, is a bureaucracy that emphasizes hierarchical controls for accountability and to maintain the status quo.

Organizationally, the SLP encompasses a variety of professional and functional areas, including wastewater treatment, dam maintenance, lab analysis, security, inspections, and record keeping. The continued and rapid growth of Spanish Lake as a recreational retreat, coupled with the surge in commercial and residential real estate, resulted in an increase in employees across the board.

THE RECORDS DEPARTMENT OF SLP

As a result of increased demand for permits and licenses, the largest growth in personnel has occurred in the Records Department of the SLP. Records at the Spanish Lake Project had always been kept in paper files with no systematic backup since the facility was built, which has led to numerous files being misplaced and increasing costs associated with tracking them down. Although previously an adequate system, the demands of an ever-growing service base have rendered the record-keeping techniques obsolete and non–cost effective. An avalanche of paper records in the form of maps, inspections, permits, and employee files has resulted in an inefficient and expensive system that requires more personnel to complete its assigned tasks than it really should. By late 2005, the office staff had ballooned to 127 employees.

At the same time, external factors such as property damage caused by Hurricane Rita and an economic downturn have led to severe shortfalls in SLP revenue. In addition, regional rivals are aggressively competing with Lake Fuerte for the area's recreational income. The overall economic forecast is also trending downward. Taking into account the predicted decline of future revenue streams, the chief executive officer of the authority, Thomas Fernandez, asked his staff to begin a reorganization of the authority that would result in a significant cost savings. Fernandez, who is appointed by the governor, is also concerned that the SLP's fiscal troubles might create a political issue for the governor who is running for reelection. He asked his staff to begin an immediate analysis to determine the least efficient units within the organization. As might be expected, the Records Office was ranked among the top of these poorly performing units within the REA.

Fernandez is considering a number of options for reorganizing the department, including eliminating it, which would annually save the authority millions of dollars. Current operations would be contracted out to a private company and any of the employees who would be retained could be transferred to other units or perhaps rehired by the company. Realizing the inevitability of at least some job reduction, the Southern Regional manager, Dave Winter, decided to form a three-person special project team to analyze and make recommendations regarding future job reduction in the Records Department. Winter, moreover, believes that it is imperative that employees of the department and the staff of SLP, in general, do not know the true purpose of this special group in advance. Therefore, each group member is instructed by Winter to, if necessary, inform inquisitive employees that the group is designed to recommend changes that will improve work conditions and bolster worker morale as a means to enhance productivity.

JAMES BLACKSTOCK

James Blackstock has spent the past ten years after college working at the Southern Region office of the Rio Estrecho Authority. Extremely loyal and hard working, James has built a reputation as an up-and-coming "company man," having risen to the position of chief financial auditor for the region. Growing up in nearby Madison County, James had always wanted to work for the REA; as soon as he graduated from the state university, he immediately went to work for the Southern Region office. Almost everyone he knew in his hometown either worked at the local branch of REA or the Spanish Lake Project, or had family that did. Ambitious, James harbored hopes of one day becoming the overall general manager of the authority.

Upon arriving for work in August 2006, James was informed of a request to attend a 9:00 a.m. meeting in the office of David Winter, his boss. Arriving at the meeting, James discovers that he was being asked to be a member of an ad hoc team of three with the responsibility for making decisions concerning reorganizing the Records Department, which would probably entail a significant reduction in workforce. The team was told that revenues were down sharply and the department needed to be streamlined and modernized. Almost in passing, Winter says that Fernandez would be pleased by a plan that "really cuts the fat" and makes the Southern Region office look good.

Already feeling conflicted and nervous that the planned reorganization might result in the laying off of old neighbors and friends, James became more dismayed when David informed him that under no circumstances was he to enlighten anyone of the actual purpose of his team. If asked, he and the other team members were to claim that they were there to determine ways to reorganize the department to make it work more effectively. In fact, they were to strongly imply that the team's objective was to save jobs and not to cut employees from the payroll. According to David, the only person at the SLP in the know about the job cuts was Ben Kraves.

Grudgingly, James accepted the assignment after his supervisor let him know that refusal to participate would seriously jeopardize his fast-track career at REA. The team would have ten days to compile and report its decision and would start the next day. Taking part in the ad hoc team with James were two fellow members of the Southern Region office, Travis Cole and Dean Burke. Travis and Dean were both new to the REA and lacked the strong personal attachment that James had with the employees from Madison and San Patricio Counties. As far they were concerned, the task was a straightforward one. James, however, remained deeply torn by the assignment. Several questions kept going through his mind as he readied himself for the assignment: What if he had to recommend letting go of a family friend or neighbor? Were other options even seriously considered—ones that might not result in wholesale layoffs? Were the cuts being made for sound financial reasons? He knew that in one way or another he would probably be acquainted with almost everyone under consideration for force reduction. Furthermore, he knew that he would have to lie to them when they asked him what his team was doing at SLP. On a personal and professional level, he felt more discomfort over this assignment than anything else he'd done in his ten years with the SLP.

Upon arrival at SLP the next day, the team got quickly to work. After a few days of observing and detailing the work process, it became clear to the members of the team that the office and Records Department were indeed overstaffed and in need of a modernized, more efficient record-keeping system. However, James was truly struck by the *esprit de corps* of the department, which he is sure would suffer greatly if jobs are cut. Moreover, the employees express their willingness to be transferred to other units if the team concludes that the SLP is truly overstaffed. It is also clear that the department's workers were totally in the dark regarding the team's true mission. The unsuspecting employees sincerely believed that James and his colleagues were interested only in improving their work conditions and saving their jobs. The whole experience was turning into an ordeal for James. Everywhere he went at the SLP, he saw someone he knew, greetings were exchanged and old tales retold; however, none of that changed the fact that changes had to be made. The problem was how to convey this to the workforce of the SLP.

Particularly troubling for James was the case of Shea Parsons, an old high school friend. James knew that it was inevitable that Shea's job in the records section of the department was slated for elimination. Complicating the situation for James was Ben Kraves, long-time friend and fishing buddy of James's father, Ron Blackstock. Ben, angry about the possible reductions in staff, had confronted James, saying, "Does your Daddy know what you're going to do to the people you have grown up with? It is shameful and I am of a right mind to tell people what you are really doing here. How do you think people like Shea are going to feed their families?" Conflicted and confused, James just walked away; after all, he had a job to do.

On August 25, having completed the evaluation process, all that remained was for the group to reach a decision. James and the other members of the ad hoc team left the SLP in the morning to arrive in time for their meeting with Winter. Driving back to the Southern Region office, James felt a sense of relief on the one hand that it was over. On the other hand, decisions still had to be made and he hoped made for the right reasons. He, however, felt a sense of regret that he could not be up front with those affected by the reduction in staff. Surely, the process could have been more transparent, James thought.

PRIVATIZATION

One of the options being considered for the SLP is to contract out its services to a private, for-profit company. This is an idea that is currently favored by some in the Southern Regional office, including David Winter. Blackstock remains skeptical because of his close ties with the workforce of the SLP and the community there. Part of the group's mission is to report back to Winter on whether the contracting-out option is viable. Winter wants to appoint an internal task force to study the feasibility of privatizing the SLP that will likely have larger ramifications for the rest of the authority. The findings from the ad hoc team will be used by the task force in making its recommendations.

Discussion Questions

1. Do you agree with Winter's decision not to reveal the purpose of the special group to the SLP? Why or why not?
2. What do you think Blackstock will recommend to the other members of the special group? Explain.
3. What types of issues should Winter's privatization task force consider? Should privatizing the SLP be done if the task force finds that savings would result?
4. What role did the political climate play in the situation? Explain.
5. Do you think the process would have been "better" had the decision making occurred at only one level of management? How did the dual layers of management complicate the situation?

APPENDIX

The Organizational Structure of the Rio Estrecho Authority

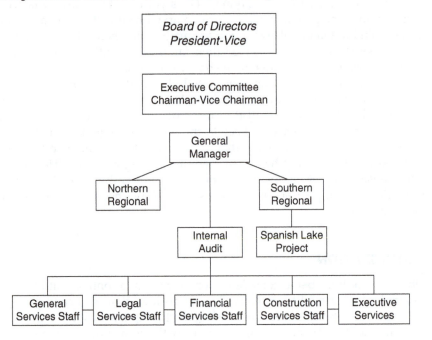

5 UNITED STATES COAST GUARD

Jennifer M. Giancola,
Robert A. Cropf, Susanne
Hoernschemeyer, and Jay Lipinski

OVERVIEW

Abstract

This case examines the bureaucratic structure and authoritarian culture of the military. Although many of these qualities allow the military to achieve its desired objectives, at other times such characteristics are a barrier. In this case, a new captain, Ron Sandura, takes control of the Coast Guard ship, the *Henry*. Ron's leadership and management style do not meet the crew's expectations in terms of positive motivation, port privileges, downtime, and so on. As tension mounts, Ron's subordinate, Clark Minneo, must decide how to handle the situation in order to prevent further decline of the crew's morale and work outcomes.

Main Topics

Leadership, Bureaucracy and structure

Secondary Topics

HR administration, Organizational culture

Teaching Purpose

To analyze culture and motivation within a military organization, and to propose suggestions for improvements in leadership and HR management

The Organization

The *Henry*, a U.S. Coast Guard river-tending ship

Main Characters

- Ron Sandura, Ship Captain
- Clark Minneo, Executive Petty Officer

BACKGROUND

The Coast Guard is the oldest continuous seagoing service in America, and it has a rich maritime tradition. As a government entity and military service, the Coast Guard has a bureaucratic structure and well-established culture that help ensure the completion of its mission. It is a highly mechanistic organization that relies on rigid policies and procedures. These characteristics do not allow much flexibility and, like other branches of the armed services, crew members must follow the orders and duties they are given.

The culture of the Coast Guard is well defined, even in its motto: Siemper Paratus (Always Ready). Some primary elements of its culture include sacrifice, stewardship, dedication to duty, compassion, leadership, selflessness, and integrity. Possibly, the most integrated aspect of this culture is the work ethic and selflessness that exist within the organization. Coast Guard members take pride in the sacrifices they make and they revel in their role as overachievers. In fact, there is an unwritten rule that prevents the members from complaining. No matter how difficult the task, no matter how long the watch, and no matter how unpleasant the situation, the crew does not complain or ask to be relieved. Although many of the traits found within the Coast Guard culture represent admirable and redeeming qualities, they also can create problems as seen in this case.

The Coast Guard has a long tradition of dedicated men and women who work extended days under harsh conditions for little pay. As a branch of the armed forces, the Coast Guard is not allowed to reward its members with monetary incentives, bonuses, overtime pay, or any other compensation of this nature. As such, it is customary in the Coast Guard to be rewarded in one of three other ways: medals/honors/awards, a pat on the back, and time off from work. These rewards are held in high regard by the members of the Coast Guard: not only as feedback on a job well done, but also as the only true addition to the basic compensations that a life of public service offers.

There are many customary ways in which these perks are doled out to Coast Guard crews. First, for Coast Guard units that spend great lengths of time at sea, there is a system known as tropical hours. This is an in-port work schedule that starts early (usually around 6:00 or 7:00 a.m.) and ends early (usually around 12:00 or 1:00 p.m.). These short days maximize the free time that Coasties have when they are in their homeport. It allows the crew to spend more time with their friends and family and make up some of the time that they spend away from home while at sea. Another method of reward is for the command of a unit to give a few days off (not vacation but just free days or "liberty"). Typically, if a ship is gone for a week or two, the captain might give a day or two of liberty to compensate for the time away from home. A cruise of a month or two might garner as much as a week or two of time off and cruises of three months or more can lead to even more compensatory time.

Individual achievements and contributions of crew members are often recognized with medals, awards, and honors. Some of these are informal and relative to the command, but others are fully sanctioned by the Coast Guard and the results are kept in the permanent records of the individuals. Other methods of compensation include shorter workdays on Fridays, special food or celebratory meals on board, morale-boosting activities (bowling, golf, a trip to the movies, etc.), and simple recognition in front of the crew for a job well done. Any or all of these forms of reward are routinely dispersed aboard Coast Guard units and they are widely recognized and accepted.

THE *HENRY*

The United States Coast Guard cutter *Henry* is a seventy-five-foot river-tending ship that is responsible for guarding and maintaining the navigable safety of more than 400 miles of the river valley. The crew of the *Henry* consists of fourteen crew members of varying age, background, experience, expertise, and tenure. The *Henry* and its crew spend an average of twelve to fifteen days per month on the rivers they patrol. When onboard, the crew works, plays, eats, sleeps, and lives together in quarters about the size of a two-bedroom apartment. In such an environment, unit morale is of the utmost importance and maintaining camaraderie is paramount to fulfilling the *Henry*'s mission. If the crew is happy, then the job gets done smoothly and efficiently. If there is any ill will or discrimination among the crew, the days run long and the work suffers.

The *Henry* crew's primary tasks, known in maritime circles as "aids to navigation," are ensuring the safe flow of commerce through America's waterways and providing guidance to both commercial and recreational boaters. The crew of the *Henry* marks the main shipping channels river with navigation buoys; builds and repairs all shore side towers and structures used for navigational aids; and identifies and charts any dangerous shoal areas or other hazards to navigation. Life aboard the *Henry* is arduous, and the work is demanding. Because of the strong culture and work ethic the crew share, this mission is carried out with equal aplomb on 100-degree summer afternoons and in driving rain and snow on frigid January mornings.

THE *HENRY'S* LEADERSHIP

The captain of the *Henry*, Ron Sandura, is a distinguished and highly decorated veteran with twenty-nine years of Coast Guard service. Sandura is noted as being a taskmaster, a disciplinarian, and an old-school leader without much of a soft side. He is notorious for working his crew for long days, hard hours, and with little time off.

During his six-month tenure as skipper of the *Henry*, Sandura has not given many awards, medals, or honors. In fact, he is not prone to thanking or congratulating the crew, and he doesn't feel obliged to give extra time off or compensatory time away from work for the crew. Sandura does not believe in tropical hours or extra liberty after a long voyage. This leadership style has led to many problems aboard the *Henry*, and the overall morale of the men has gradually declined since Sandura took command of the ship.

For the experienced personnel aboard the ship, many of Sandura's tactics run contrary to what they have encountered over the years. For the junior members aboard the *Henry*, it has been a rude awakening—not what most of them signed up for at the recruiter's office. The veteran Coasties have soured and lost their drive. Several of the novice Coasties have become disgruntled, rebellious, and restless. There are now discipline problems, requests for transfer, and attempts to leave the Coast Guard early, just to avoid being under Sandura's command.

Captain Sandura is not the only player on the *Henry*. Although he has the autonomy to make most of the decisions concerning the command of his vessel, he has a command team that works beside him to run the day-to-day operations of the ship. Clark Minneo is the executive petty officer, the second in command and right hand man to Captain Sandura. He personally regulates the workflow and the climate aboard the *Henry* as much if not more than Sandura. Minneo is responsible for establishing the work list for all departments, ordering supplies, making financial decisions, deciding on matters such as sick leave and vacation, and dispensing punishment and discipline when necessary. He ultimately sets the tone and the mood aboard the ship.

Minneo and Captain Sandura have a cordial working relationship. Minneo is a rank below Sandura, but he has more direct experience and leadership credentials than the captain. This has been a sore spot for Minneo since Sandura became captain. Minneo believes that Sandura was appointed for political reasons without use of a fair hiring process. Furthermore, neither Minneo nor the other crew members were consulted when the captain's position became available. Although Minneo believes that he is more qualified than Sandura, he knows better than to challenge the system. He made the decision from the start to put his feelings aside for the betterment of the *Henry* and its crew, and he treats Sandura and his authority with respect.

CAPTAIN V. CREW

This summer, the crew of the *Henry* set out on a particularly hot Monday morning, heading up the river on an excursion to service aids to navigation and to make any necessary repairs and adjustments to the existing structures along the river. The trip took the crew of the *Henry* eleven days round trip. This was the first lengthy trip that the crew had taken under Sandura's command. Crew members did not know exactly what to expect, but they were hopeful that it would mirror past trips that they had on the *Henry* under different command.

One of the benefits of being aboard a river tender, as opposed to a seagoing vessel, is that the work cannot be done at night. Navigating the river at night is one thing, but setting 1,500-pound buoys and climbing towers along the bank is a whole different story. Because the crew could not work at night, the *Henry* usually pulled into a port, a town, or at least to the side of the river every evening and stayed put until first light the next day. This gave the crew a chance to get off of the boat to go for a walk or even see a movie, depending on where the *Henry* docked. The crew worked hard all day and greatly appreciated this personal time when the day was done. This was recognized and accepted behavior in the river-tender community, and the crew of the *Henry* expected it. Along the *Henry*'s route were several towns that had the facilities to accommodate a large ship such as the *Henry* for the evening. Many of these towns also had distractions and amenities that the crew enjoyed. There were enough of these towns that on any given night, the captain could take his pick of ports.

On this trip, however, Sandura did something contrary to the accepted norm: he seemingly went out of his way to stop the *Henry* each evening a few miles above or a few miles below any towns along the bank. He chose places that, although suitable for the ship to anchor, did not allow for any recreation for the crew. Some of the stopping points were so isolated that the crew could not even exit the ship once moored. The members of the crew started to grumble among themselves. They had been working diligently and had completed every task asked of them on this trip. *Why was the captain not giving them the one perk that he had the power to give?*

As the trip progressed, Sandura continued to forgo the ritual of spending the night in port and proceeded to find various uninhabitable locales along the river. The morale of the crew was visibly affected. There was infighting, bickering among shipmates, lethargy, and a general uneasiness that was not normal aboard the *Henry*.

On the eleventh day of the journey, the *Henry* slipped back into its home-port, having covered more than 400 miles of river. The crew had placed more than seventy navigational buoys along the route and effected repairs to more than twenty shore-side structures. The temperatures had been in the nineties and the humidity had made the air thick enough to cut with a knife, but the members of the crew had performed their jobs in typical Coast Guard fashion.

Upon returning to port, the crew is required to perform numerous ritualized tasks before anyone is allowed to go home. These include washing the ship from top to bottom, offloading expended supplies, refueling, and writing reports that are required by headquarters. Another longstanding tradition upon returning from a mission is known as "quarters." Quarters takes place after all of the mundane returning tasks are completed. The crew of the ship gathers to discuss the trip it just completed. Crew members highlight any lessons learned, recall any close calls or safety concerns, and set the stage for the next mission. This is also a time for the captain to recognize the hard work and dedication of any or all of the crew members. Since the crew members do not get overtime pay, bonuses, merit raises, or any other form of compensation, this praise in front of their shipmates is important to morale.

During quarters for the preceding *Henry* mission, Sandura did not say a word apart from the review of the work done and some minor details regarding the next trip. Crew members were left wondering what they had done wrong on their mission that had made the captain act so abnormally harsh.

THE LAST STRAW

After the crew broke from quarters, Minneo briefed them about when they had to report back to the ship for work. It is an unwritten rule in the Coast Guard that the crew should usually expect a day or two off after a ten- or eleven-day trip with no breaks. Clark announced to the crew that they were all to report back to work the very next day to resume in-port duties. They were not to receive any extra time off—a decision that, although presented by Minneo, had Sandura's fingerprints all over it. There would be no free time during the excursion, no pats on the back upon return, and no liberty for a job well done. The crew members were dumbfounded. Some shook their heads in disbelief, some sighed in disgust, and others had to muffle their shouts of anger. Although everyone was angry, no one aboard the *Henry* had the fortitude to question Sandura's tactics, and no one on the command team stood up for the crew.

This trend continued for the next several months, and the morale and drive of the crew members continued to plummet. There was no recognition, no extra liberty, no port calls, and no tropical hours. Instead, the crew received days and days of hot, backbreaking work for a wage that barely kept them above the poverty level. In spite of the obvious effects that this was having on the crew, Sandura did not waiver in his leadership style or in his decision making when it came to matters of the crew.

Minneo knew things were not going well. He was well aware that the crew's expectations were not being met, but for some time neither he nor anyone else on the command staff did anything to influence the captain's decisions. In a culture where everyone must pull his or her own weight and there is nowhere to hide when the work begins, Sandura's leadership style went unchecked. No one complained directly to the command and the work continued to get done. The usual perks offered to the crew of a Coast Guard vessel were unofficial, not guaranteed. Under Captain Sandura, they were not even considered.

Eventually, even Minneo becomes impatient with Sandura. Even though he is a senior officer and has to set an example for the crew, Minneo wants to spend some time with his family and away from the boat. After a particularly hot, humid, and exhausting trip in August, Minneo decides to go to the captain's chambers to discuss the situation.

Discussion Questions

1. How do you think Minneo should respond to the crew members? Should he give his input to the captain about what the crew expects?

2. How can the command team, and/or the Coast Guard in general, motivate the crew of a ship? Should the informal perks be written into the standing

orders of the ship or formalized in some fashion to prevent the uncertainty the crew of the *Henry* experienced?

3. Is a bureaucratic/mechanistic structure still the best option for the military in today's environment? Describe the current structure and design elements and suggest changes, if appropriate.

4. What type of power base and leadership style does Captain Sandura possess? Based on leadership theory and research, create a leadership development plan for him.

5. How do the operations and culture of a military organization differ from other types of organizations, that is, nonprofit, public, and/or private? Do you think these differences are warranted by the types of extreme situations these organizations must face?

6 | SOUTHERN MEDICAL SCHOOL

Jennifer M. Giancola,
Robert A. Cropf, and
Michaele L. Hall

OVERVIEW

Abstract

This case examines the misalignment among the structure, culture, strategy, and environment in a nonprofit university. Specifically, the Division of Plastic Surgery within Southern Medical School operates with a different structure and culture than the rest of the university and medical school. Furthermore, the nature of academic medicine requires that strict policies and procedures are followed. In this case, problems ensue when Dr. Larry Smith decides to follow his own procedures for what he believes is the best interest of the patient. By not complying with billing policies, his actions create an ethical dilemma for the division and the medical school.

Main Topics

Bureaucracy and structure, Ethics

Secondary Topics

Organizational culture, Communication

Teaching Purpose

To demonstrate how misalignment of structure, culture, and environment within an organization can lead to problems in communication and decision making, and ultimately contribute to unethical behavior.

The Organization

The case examines the Division of Plastic Surgery within Southern Medical School, a nonprofit division within a university hospital.

Main Characters

- Dr. Larry Smith, Medical Doctor and Faculty Member
- Jan Ellendale, Reimbursement Manager
- Michael James, Business Director

BACKGROUND

The Division of Plastic Surgery at Southern University Medical School is part of one of the top nonprofit medical schools in the United States. Southern has a number of specialty areas, including cardiac surgery, neurology, plastic surgery, and pediatric oncology. The Division of Plastic Surgery, in particular, has a competitive residency program, and like most of the medical school divisions, employs the top practitioners in the field. Southern is associated with a premier hospital for both children and adults, providing a wide range of opportunities for teaching and innovation in the field of plastic surgery.

No matter how many qualified medical professionals a school employs, an organization that practices medicine needs more than just physicians. There are people to be healed, but there are also business operations to be managed, rules to be followed, regulations to be met, bills to be paid, and government programs to be navigated. The Division of Plastic Surgery employs a number of medical assistants, secretaries, and a complete billing staff to support the practitioners at the university hospital.

ORGANIZATIONAL STRUCTURE

Southern University, for the most part, is a bureaucracy with a strict hierarchy and top-down decision making to the various schools and colleges. The medical school is subject not only to the university's policies and procedures, but also to those of the hospital as well as government regulations. Nonetheless, the medical school's structure resembles a matrix organization more than a traditional hierarchy: most employees report to more than one superior. For example, a staff member employed in the billing department of the Division of Plastic Surgery may report to both the business director and the division's physicians. The physicians themselves may report to more than one superior such as the department chair and their specialist director. The structure allows the medical school to manage the demands of its diverse students, physicians, divisions, and employees.

The medical school has a high level of horizontal differentiation. In the Division of Plastic Surgery, there is a department for adult specialists and pediatric specialists, and subgroups for specialists in different areas (e.g., hand, facial, nerve). The division has its own business director and staff as well as administrative assistants who are stationed within the department. Figure 1 depicts the division's organizational structure.

Decision making in the medical school is fairly decentralized. Whereas the dean and division chiefs make some of the decisions, most of the day-to-day decisions are made by the people who are doing the actual work. Physicians in a division implement various policies and procedures, as do the supervisors of each billing group. The decisions that are made at the lower levels affect only a specific division or a few divisions confronting similar issues. Furthermore, the physicians are accustomed to working independently to conduct research within their specialization and serve a particular type of patient.

The high level of differentiation and decentralization leads to problems in both a vertical and a horizontal direction. Although the divisions are interdependent in areas such as finances and patient care, there is a lack of communication and integration across and within divisions. As a result, resources are not shared adequately, and there is a loss of economies of scale and scope. Since many policies and procedures are not effectively communicated in a downward direction as necessary, there is a lack of consistency in delivering patient care. It is difficult to implement and enforce policies and procedures. Furthermore, divisions fail to share best practices and lessons learned, and organizational learning does not occur.

ORGANIZATIONAL CULTURE

An academic medical setting has a different culture from other types of medical settings. In addition to patient care, teaching and research are expected and highly valued. Physicians carry clinical loads in the hospital, teach medical students, and conduct research. A culture of learning is supported by faculty-student mentoring, state-of-the-art research labs, and faculty development workshops. Faculty members are rewarded for teaching excellence and scholarly productivity.

University and medical school cultures also reflect a highly bureaucratic structure with rigid policies and procedures. Physicians in an academic setting are required to abide by different rules than physicians in a group practice or a private practice, especially when it comes to billing practices. Teaching physicians are regulated by the government, the medical community, and the university itself. Because of the federal regulations, many medical schools have set up even more stringent guidelines for their physicians to follow. As a result, the employees in the Division of Plastic Surgery must act within a strict set of rules that sometimes conflicts with aspects of their culture.

Cultures vary among the divisions at the medical school. Whereas most divisions focus on quality patient outcomes, individualized and responsive patient care are key values for the Division of Plastic Surgery. Staff and physicians must be adaptable and available to meet the needs of a heavy patient load. Staff must be ready to assist the patients and physicians at all times. The physicians must focus on the unique needs of each patient who is often looking for noncritical surgery that can enhance his/her appearance. The patient may be nervous and looking for the best one-on-one attention possible. The multiple responsibilities are demanding for the faculty members, who frequently complain about juggling patients, students, and research.

The Division of Plastic Surgery also looks a lot different from other medical school divisions. The focus on aesthetics is evident in the division's environment as well. The plastic surgery suite has a lovely ambiance, including attractive lighting, artwork, and overall elegant fixtures and décor, that reinforces a culture that values beauty as well as healing.

A decentralized, horizontally differentiated organization can find itself with a fragmented culture. Within the Division of Plastic Surgery are many different personalities with their own sets of values and norms that they learned from their parents, siblings, friends, and mentors. They do share one common value: helping people. No one goes into the medical field, especially a teaching facility, unless he/she wants to help others. If such a person does not have this value, he/she does not last very long in the division.

THE CASE OF DOCTOR SMITH

Dr. Larry Smith is one of the best face specialists in the country and loves his work. Taking care of patients is a number one priority for him. In fact, he is known for spending long hours with patients and taking on more patients than he can handle. He particularly enjoys working with patients with facial abnormalities or injuries that require special reconstructive surgery. As a child, Larry had a close friend who was injured in a car accident resulting in visible disfigurement. Watching his friend deal with ridicule from classmates encouraged Larry to enter this specialty and make a difference for others. Over the years, he has taken on numerous pro bono cases.

Dr. Smith never seems to mind the hours or making sacrifices in his personal life. He is well respected and colleagues frequently go to him with questions. Medical students from around the country seek him out as a mentor.

A highly desirable specialist, Dr. Smith has a very tight schedule in which he has to fit office visits, teaching, consultation, and surgery. To facilitate scheduling, Dr. Smith tries to set aside specific days for surgery, and on these days he tries to schedule enough cases to minimize downtime. Sometimes, however, there are surprises and emergencies that require his attention.

EMERGENCY DILEMMA

On October 29, Dr. Smith had a typical day scheduled in the operating room until an emergency case arrived at 6:00 a.m. None of the on-call physicians stepped forward to take on the case except for Dr. Smith. The surgery began at 6:30 a.m. and lasted 12 hours. Given that he had the best residents and fellows assisting that day, Dr. Smith felt comfortable conducting his previously scheduled surgeries as well. If he had canceled, it might have taken weeks for his other patients to get rescheduled. Hence, he ran back and forth between the rooms, overseeing the work of the residents and fellows. Dr. Smith was able to complete all of the surgeries scheduled for the day in addition to the emergency case.

Although Dr. Smith's actions were in line with federal guidelines, he went against the medical school's policy. The policy specifies that a physician must be present during the critical portion of a procedure and may not perform more than two procedures in an overlapping time period. During the noncritical portions of the procedure, the teaching physician must be immediately available (free from any other critical activity) to return to the teaching setting or must designate by name a second teaching physician who is immediately available. Dr. Smith knew that he had acted contrary to the medical school's policy. But in Dr. Smith's mind, this method provided the greatest good to the greatest number of people while also keeping the schedule running smoothly.

Many of Dr. Smith's colleagues also think that this policy is absurd. They believe that they are able to run more than two operating rooms at one time and that they should not have to adhere to policies that exceed federal guidelines and are made by nonphysicians. This can cause a somewhat volatile atmosphere between physicians and compliance personnel at the medical school. Tension between outside rules and division culture are even more pronounced in the Division of Plastic Surgery, where those who should follow the rules and those who should enforce them work closely together. Unfortunately, the physicians sometimes think that the rules they have to work under are keeping them from fulfilling the Hippocratic oath. Because of these issues, there are times when a doctor will stretch the limits of the rules. When doctors are caught doing so, they become angry with the messenger who has to enforce the rules and with the system that requires them.

BILLING ISSUES

Dr. Smith was a great physician, but he had a bad habit of turning in his billing papers late. Billing for surgeries required that a sheet be submitted with the physician's charge for the surgery, which was then coded and posted. The billing staff usually did most of this for Dr. Smith. By the time he submitted the charges for all of the surgeries, the cases had already been billed even though Dr. Smith wrote on his charge sheet not to bill for the emergency surgery. Dr. Smith had unilaterally decided to do the case pro bono for a number of reasons, including evading the medical school's policy on number of surgeries allowed.

At this point, Jan Ellendale, reimbursement manger, became suspicious and began checking into all five of the surgeries performed that day to see if the proper procedures and rules were followed. She discovered that in Dr. Smith's operative notes, the doctor stated that he had been in each operating room for the entire duration of the surgery. Since this would have been physically impossible, Ellendale knew that by billing any of the services, the school would be committing fraud. She brought the situation to the attention of the business director, Michael James. He agreed that something fishy was going on, but he was unsure how to handle it. The situation was compounded by the fact that Dr. Smith did not report to him, and he had seniority in the school.

James scheduled a meeting in which Dr. Smith was brought in to discuss the cases in question and to explain what had happened. Dr. Smith was very angry about the situation and offended that James would question him. He felt that he was the best physician to oversee the emergency surgery, and none of the other physicians wanted to do it. He argued that he did nothing wrong. Although he stepped out of the emergency case, there were other physicians within the practice who could have been immediately available if one of the residents had an urgent question. Dr. Smith chose to change his presence statement in the operative report so that he could address all of his patients' needs.

What Dr. Smith had done was against the university's reimbursement code but did not cause any physical harm to any patients. The billing and reimbursement offices, however, were now aware of what had occurred. They were legitimately worried that Dr. Smith had done this in the past and suspected that he would continue to do so. They were also worried that this was becoming a common practice in that division as physicians tried to maximize their caseloads. They had no choice but to report him to the university ethics board.

While investigating the situation, a second issue also caught the attention of the ethics board. The emergency surgery was taking place at a hospital satellite site at least two miles away from the other four surgeries. Although nothing happened this time, supervising surgeries at such distant locations poses risks to patients that extend beyond billing questions. Dr. Smith's behavior did not seem consistent with the Hippocratic oath he so valued and which compelled him to put the health of his patients first.

A PERVASIVE PROBLEM

James decided to investigate the issue further with other physicians to see if this was a pervasive problem. The findings were not good: often the main surgeons popped in and out multiple times during long, arduous surgeries, letting residents do the grunt work. The residents were all highly capable, but the legal fact remained that the university would be committing fraud if it pretended that the presiding physicians were constantly present during these operations.

James and Ellendale were stuck: they knew the practices going on in the Division of Plastic Surgery were contrary to university rules and potentially even harmful to patients, but they did not know exactly where to start addressing the problem. The matrix structure of the university only compounded this problem, given that some superiors may have been engaging in the same kinds of practices. At the same time, the residents were getting valuable experience, fulfilling the university's teaching mission. Enforcing billing constraints on physicians could reduce the depth of the educational experience available to students. Not only could their hands-on time be diminished, but giving the university a reputation of being an uncooperative place to work could also reduce the school's long-term appeal to top students and practitioners.

Discussion Questions

1. What are the ethical dilemmas at work in this case?
2. How might the division and medical school support an environment of consistent ethical decision making?

3. How did the structure and culture of the medical school and the Division of Plastic Surgery contribute to the situation and Dr. Smith's behavior? What changes are needed?

4. What suggestions would you make regarding how to improve vertical and horizontal communication and integration at the medical school?

5. What actions would you recommend that the business director and the ethics board take?

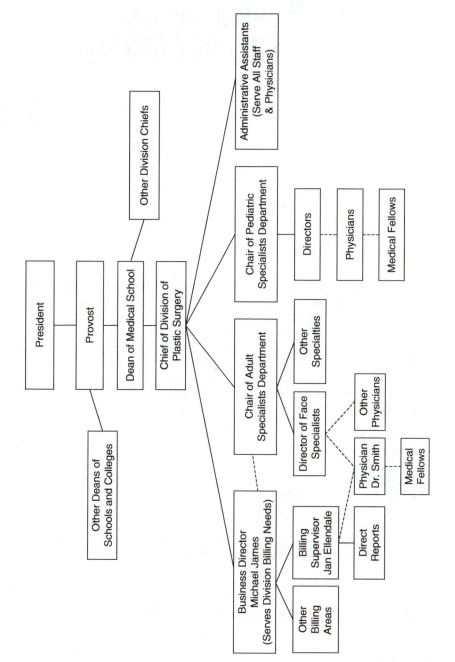

7

CRIME VICTIM SUPPORT CENTER

Jennifer M. Giancola,
Robert A. Cropf, and
Jessica Vick

OVERVIEW

Abstract

This case involves the Crime Victim Support Center (CVSC), a nonprofit organization that helps the victims of crime by acting as an advocate for their interests. It examines client conflict of interest that develops when a caseworker at the agency, Laura Green, must decide whether to represent separately an estranged mother and father who are seeking resolution concerning the death of their son. Lacking a definitive policy directive from the organization, the caseworker must decide how to balance the best interests of both her clients and the organization she represents. Working with her supervisor, the caseworker attempts to navigate this uncharted territory and reach a resolution that is satisfactory to all involved parties.

Main Topic

Decision making

Secondary Topics

Ethics, Bureaucracy and structure

Teaching Purpose

To explore the ethical dilemmas in resolving a case of competing client interests; and to discuss organizational decision making and nonprofit administration.

The Organization

The Crime Victims Support Center (CVSC) is a nonprofit organization that helps the victims of crime by acting as an advocate for their interests.

Main Characters

- Laura Green, Victims Advocate
- Christine Hayden, Executive Director
- John and Catherine Taft, Clients

BACKGROUND

Situated in a small office in midtown, the Crime Victim Support Center (CVSC) serves victims of *any* type of crime, regardless of the case's criminal justice system status. This makes it unique among victim service agencies in the area. Other agencies, such as Parents of Murdered Children and Legal Advocates for Abused Women, serve victims of specific crimes. The prosecuting attorneys' offices at the city, county, and federal levels of the courts serve victims whose cases are being prosecuted. CVSC therefore holds the distinction of being the only agency in the Midwest that serves victims of physical and property crimes, regardless of whether the crime was reported or an arrest has been made.

CVSC was founded in 1979 with a goal of protecting victims who, until that point, had no agencies to officially advocate on their behalf. Through the intervening years, CVSC honed its mission statement and set the following goals: helping victims through direct service; changing the way the public treats victims through public advocacy; and contributing to the knowledge of victim issues for other professionals through training and technical assistance.

CVSC employs a staff of four daytime victim advocates, a volunteer coordinator, a licensed counselor, an executive director, and five after-hours advocates. The agency runs a 24-hour hotline for victims in crisis. Victim advocates are in the office from 8:30 a.m. to 5:00 p.m. and maintain a caseload of crime victims and their families for services such as referrals to community agencies, professional counseling, and personal advocacy. They are responsible for returning calls taken by the after-hours advocates when the office is closed. CVSC's advocates strive to meet the needs of the clients that occur as a result of the crime. These vary widely from the need for clothing or food after a burglary to the need for funeral assistance after a homicide. One of the most common resources to which CVSC staff refers its clients is Midwest Crime Victims' Compensation.

MIDWEST CRIME VICTIMS' COMPENSATION

In 1981, the state government enacted the Midwest Crime Victims' Compensation Act. As part of that legislation, the Victims' Compensation Fund was created. This program, supported through offender-generated court costs and seizures, provides reimbursement or payment for funeral expenses and/or medical expenses, lost wages, or loss of support for children and dependents. If a victim or victim's family members meet the requirements, which include reporting the crime to law enforcement within 48 hours and cooperating with prosecution, they may be eligible for this fund. The fund is administered by the Division of Worker's Compensation. Although this state agency is separate from the Crime Victim Support Center, CVSC advocates assist their clients in filing for compensation by: explaining the program; providing the application form; helping to fill out the paperwork; giving them access to the agency's free notary public; and advocating for them throughout the process.

Victims' Compensation has been invaluable to many of CVSC's clients who would be burdened with thousands of dollars in medical or funeral expenses. This available money, however, can occasionally cause problems or hard feelings among family and friends who may not know who is eligible or how the system works. CVSC advocates often encounter multiple members of victims' families who want to know whether they are entitled to money from the fund. Such cases include divorced parents or children by multiple mothers. These conversations require tact and skill without breaking confidentiality of other clients and without discouraging potentially eligible recipients from applying. One such case is the Taft family.

THE TAFT FAMILY CASE

John and Catherine Taft met in their teens. By the time they were both in their 20s, they had married and started a family. Their youngest son, Derrick, was born five years into the marriage. The family of John, Catherine, Derrick, and his two older sisters resided in an old bungalow on the city's south side.

A year after Derrick was born, cracks in his parents' marriage began to show. They often fought about how to spend the little extra money they had. Accusations of financial misconduct from both spouses were common and eventually the stress became too much for the marriage to support. Just before Derrick's second birthday, his parents divorced. John and Catherine rarely spoke in the intervening years. As soon as Derrick turned 18, he left his mother's house and moved out on his own. His parents worried about him, but he assured them that he and his new girlfriend were making a home for themselves with her parents, and they were thinking of starting a family.

Soon after moving out, Derrick was murdered in an alley in the city on a Friday night. He was stabbed several times, and there were neither witnesses nor suspects on the scene. His parents were both notified of their son's death by the police early on Saturday morning.

After dealing with the initial shock, John and Catherine met at a local funeral home to begin making arrangements for their son. The potential cost of the funeral only added to their pain, and they began arguing in front of the funeral director. The funeral director suggested that they contact CVSC for assistance. Within hours, John and Catherine Taft separately called the 24-hour hotline for the Crime Victim Support Center. They each spoke to the after-hours advocate who explained CVSC's services and promised that a victim advocate would call them back on Monday morning.

LAURA GREEN'S DILEMMA

Laura Green, a full-time victim advocate for CVSC, came across her job almost by accident. As an aimless undergrad searching for an internship and possessing a penchant for social causes, she was intrigued by the option of working with victims of crime rather than offenders. She enjoyed the blend of social work and social justice and quickly became close with the other employees of the agency. Impressed with the agency's mission of justice and eager to get job experience, Laura continued to volunteer after graduation.

Although disheartened by the difficulty she had finding employment after college, Laura remained dedicated to the cause of crime victim services and the prospect of employment in that field. When one of CVSC's advocates left the agency for a new position, Laura was offered the job and she quickly accepted. Several years later, Laura is still proud of her job and still dedicated to the mission of CVSC.

Laura was the first advocate into the office Monday morning. She received the message from the after-hours advocate explaining that John and Catherine's son had been murdered and that both members of the divorced couple were looking for assistance. She also mentioned to Laura that Ms. Taft hinted at financial difficulties in the couple's past and that it could be a potential concern for the advocate who took on the case.

Laura realized that an important decision had to be made: turn away one of the parents; turn one of the parents over to a different advocate; or take on both parents herself. In trying to make a decision, Laura looked through CVSC's policies and training material, but she could not find anything on dealing with this type of competing client interests. Next, she decided to refer to the CVSC Code of Ethics. After searching high and low for the code, she finally found an old copy in a file. Again, it did not provide information specific to this situation. Laura decided that she should meet with the CVSC executive director, Christine Hayden, to discuss the Taft case.

MEETING BETWEEN LAURA AND CHRISTINE

Christine was a recent transplant to CVSC. After the agency's long-time executive director retired, Christine was hired by the Board of Directors in hopes that she could turn around the flailing center. Christine possessed a postgraduate educational background of corporate management, communications, and leadership studies along with an eagerness to learn more about the victim services field. Her dedication and strong business background took the agency from the brink of closure to a surviving, if not thriving, service provider in just over a year. She also had learned much about the agency's workings, although the specifics of every CVSC resource were still not clear. She was never afraid to ask a question or to hear a truthful answer.

Christine and Laura had immediately formed a bond over a shared love of politics, sports, and a healthy debate on both. Although Laura was several years younger than Christine, she felt that her boss respected her opinion and she respected Christine's experience.

Laura walked into Christine's office from the common room she shared with the other advocates. She tapped lightly on the door to announce her presence. "What can I do for you?" Christine asked.

"We got a call on the hotline over the weekend from two divorced parents whose son was murdered. Apparently, they are not on the best terms and both want to work with our agency. I would like to get your insight," Laura explained.

Christine looked puzzled, "Don't we have a policy in place for this? It can't be the first time this has come up."

"Well, it's not the first time, but it's always been an on-the-fly decision," Laura admitted.

Christine then asked, "I'm surprised there isn't a plan in place to make these choices. First and foremost, we should not turn either of them away. So, we have to decide the best way to help them both. What are the biggest concerns about having them both with one advocate?"

"Well," Laura began, "If I take on both cases, I can track their progress simultaneously to make sure they are both being told the same things and to make sure I am aware of the individual problems as they come up."

"But?" Christine prodded.

"I don't want one parent to find out that I am working with both of them and for that to cause a problem," Laura said.

"I can see how that could potentially cause problems for the agency. The last thing we or our financial supporters want is to give the impression that we're being dishonest or biased. You could tell them that you are not able to comment on who is or is not a client of the agency and that could cover you if something comes up later. What about you, personally? How does it make you feel to think about working with both parents?"

"The last thing I want is for our agency to make this an even more negative experience for them. Their son was murdered. I want to help them both as much as possible. I worry that if they find out I am working with both spouses, they would feel betrayed, and it might discourage them from filing for compensation or for coming in for counseling. Ethically, I don't want to do anything that would potentially compromise our relationship and prevent them from accessing all the services to which they are entitled," Laura said, looking concerned.

"That's a valid concern. The last thing I want is for you to compromise your ethics. What else?" Christine prodded.

"I also worry about being put in a compromising position, where one parent is looking for information on the other or looking for me to give them some advantage over the spouse for obtaining services," Laura admitted.

"Do we know what services they want?" Christine asked.

"I believe they are both calling for Victims' Compensation for the funeral costs since they had no life insurance. It would probably help to have them both as my clients if they are both filing for compensation," Laura mused, working through her thoughts out loud.

"Why is that?" Christine inquired.

Laura took this as an opportunity to give her executive director an insight on the workings of the Midwest Crime Victim's Compensation program. "The person who signs the contract with the funeral home for services is the person who can apply for compensation. If I have them both as my clients, then I can make sure to tell them the exact same thing. If they don't trust their former spouse to give them the money back if they are awarded, then they should make sure to be cosigners on the funeral bill. That way, I'm sure they both have the information in the first conversation. I think that would be easier for me and probably more helpful for the clients. Although, if they both wanted to come in for notary on the same day, that could definitely cause a conflict or breach of confidentiality."

"I can see how it would be efficient to have one person delivering the message to both clients. It also seems like a fine line for one advocate to walk. What happens if they are not awarded?"

"I would try to prepare them for that like I would with any other clients. I would let them know that by being cosigners, they are both taking legal responsibility for paying the bill. Also, I always let my clients know what might disqualify them; if the victim was convicted of two or more felonies; if he was in the act of committing a crime when he was victimized; all of those. Most important, I always stress to them that the ultimate decision on whether clients are awarded compensation is not CVSC's. Still, if one's awarded and the other is not, I would hate to think that they might suspect our agency had something to do with the decision."

Christine went quiet for a minute, obviously considering the options before her. Then she said, "It sounds like you have a handle on this case and it would be better for you to take both parents. You can make sure that they both have the information they need, and understand that our agency is here to help with the forms and provide other services, but that we work under confidentiality and are not responsible for the Victims' Compensation decision. As long as you feel you can ethically work with both, I think it's the right decision. Please let me know if you have any problems or if, after talking to them, you think we made the wrong decision. The last thing I want is to put you in an uncomfortable situation. We could always transfer one client to another advocate."

Laura responded, "I believe it's in the Tafts' best interest to have one victim advocate work with both of them. Ethically, as long as I know I have done everything I can to ensure the best outcome for both clients, I can work with them. If one expressly states that he or she wants a separate victim advocate from the other, we can cross that bridge at that time. Like you said, I can always transfer a case." She thanked Christine for her help and went back to the outer office to make her calls.

THE DECISION IN ACTION

Laura carefully dialed the number for Catherine Taft. When Ms. Taft answered, Laura explained who she was and asked what kind of help Ms. Taft needed. As the after-hours advocate had stated, Catherine Taft's teenage son was found stabbed to death over the weekend. She had not finalized the funeral arrangements but planned to do so with her ex-husband later that day. Laura explained that Victims' Compensation might be able to reimburse or pay out up to $5,000 in funeral expenses if the family qualified. At that point,

Catherine Taft mentioned that she and her former husband had been divorced for several years and that they had a history of money problems. She was adamant that she did not trust him to reimburse her for her out-of-pocket costs if he were awarded money for the funeral. She also told Laura that she believed her husband would be calling CVSC.

Laura was careful to explain to Ms. Taft that if she wanted to be sure she could file for compensation, then she would need to sign the funeral bill. And, if she and her husband both signed the bill, then they could apply independently. Laura also informed her new client that no member of the agency's staff could comment on whether her husband was receiving services from the agency. To be certain Ms. Taft understood CVSC's role in the compensation process, Laura explained that she and her agency did not make the decision of who would be awarded compensation. They also did not make the decision of who deserved to apply. She told Ms. Taft that if her husband called, then he would likely receive the application as well. The best solution was to make sure they both signed for the funeral. Catherine Taft indicated that she understood.

Laura let Catherine Taft know that she would send the Victims' Compensation form to her along with information on her rights as a family member of a crime victim and information on CVSC's counseling program and support group. Laura asked her client to call if there were any problems or if the funeral home had any questions she could not answer. She also told Ms. Taft that she would keep in touch over the application process.

Within fifteen minutes of Laura's conversation with Catherine Taft, her former husband, John Taft, called CVSC. Laura explained the same information to Mr. Taft as she had discussed with his former spouse. Laura explained Victims' Compensation's policy on who can apply and informed Mr. Taft that either he or his ex-wife could sign and pay back the other if awarded, or they could both sign and individually apply with their own receipts. She was careful to stress the agency's policy of confidentiality and the policy of serving as many members of a family as call for services.

Mr. Taft became very upset. He had spoken to Catherine and knew that she had already discussed the situation with Laura. Apparently, Catherine had contacted John immediately after hanging up with Laura. Mr. Taft also was concerned about ensuring that he was reimbursed for the money he expected to pay out of pocket for his son's funeral. He told Laura that Catherine had an ongoing alcohol problem and could not be trusted. He believed that it was a conflict of interest for Laura to be working with both of them and that Laura was being deceptive. Mr. Taft demanded to speak with "someone in charge."

Discussion Questions

1. Do you agree with the way in which Laura and Christine chose to handle the Taft case? Does CVSC have an obligation to work with both clients?
2. How can CVSC diffuse Mr. Taft's anger and effectively resolve the situation?

3. What are the strengths and weaknesses of the decision-making approach that Christine used with Laura?

4. How did CVSC's policies and procedures, or lack thereof, contribute to the problem? What does CVSC need to do to successfully handle these types of situations in the future?

5. What are the ethical dilemmas in the case? How can CVSC better promote ethical standards within its work environment?

8 UNIVERSITY PHONE CENTER CASE

Jennifer M. Giancola,
Robert A. Cropf, and
Rebecca Aune

OVERVIEW

Abstract

This case examines the impact of organizational change on employee motivation and organizational culture. Specifically, the Annual Giving Department in a state public university must make changes that will allow it to reach higher fund-raising goals in the Phone Center. The Phone Center was running smoothly until Robert Kinbote, the new assistant director, was hired and began to alter the rules and atmosphere of the department. Now, the supervisors and their direct reports are dissatisfied with the work environment. Phone Supervisor Rachel, in particular, is clashing with Robert and is conflicted about how to handle the situation.

Main Topics

Leadership, Human resource administration

Secondary Topic

Organizational culture

Teaching Purpose

To examine the fit among leadership styles, organizational goals, and employee motivation, and how change can clash with the culture and impact employee morale.

The Organization

The case examines a phone center in a fund-raising department at a state university.

Main Characters

- Amelia McKenzie, Director of Annual Giving
- Robert Kinbote, Assistant Director of Annual Giving
- Rachel Hewett, Phone Center Supervisor

BACKGROUND

The University of Southern Phone Center is a subdivision of the Annual Giving Department, the functional area in charge of university fund-raising. The Phone Center employs university students who call up to 40,000 alumni each year to solicit donations, which account for the majority of all pledges made each year. The Phone Center is an intimate organization with a small number of student fund-raisers and supervisors. Team morale is especially important because callers have to enthusiastically sell the idea of donating to the university to get results. The Phone Center has fund-raising goals that must be met each year. Goals include a total donation target, the number of alums who donate, and increasing donation amounts of previous donors.

PHONE CENTER ENVIRONMENT

Until six months ago, the Phone Center consisted of a hierarchy of positions that was quite simple: director of annual giving (Amelia), Phone Center supervisors (Rachel, Jesse, Christine, and Jeremy), and fund-raisers (various university students). Daily shifts at the Phone Center were managed by one of the four supervisors, each of them working three shifts per week. Amelia oversaw the supervisors, who in turn submitted a nightly report and attended a weekly meeting. Before beginning the application process for a position as supervisor, students had to be fund-raisers for at least two consecutive semesters. Therefore, each of the four student supervisors had previously done fund-raising for the Phone Center and knew what it took to get results.

The supervisors were given the autonomy to create motivational techniques and incentives for success, monitor calls and coach fund-raisers, and set goals and follow-up schedules with each of the fund-raisers who worked under them. Amelia trusted the supervisors to use their discretion on discipline, attendance, and coaching matters. She relied on them to follow Phone Center policies to the best of their knowledge. Amelia worked during the days, but since the students also made calls in the evening, it became the student supervisors' responsibility to do all of the statistical reporting from the shift and to keep track of attendance and time cards. Because the supervisors had autonomy and independence, their work procedures and expectations were not strictly defined and they exercised creativity in decision making and coaching.

There was a strong rapport among Amelia, the supervisors, and the student fund-raisers. When hired, students were introduced to everyone and socially integrated into the department. Introductions and "get to know you" games were organized at the beginning of every shift. There was friendly competition between teams when games were played and between individuals when bonus incentives were at stake. The supervisors developed the games and competitions to address the areas that could be improved in the Phone Center and the goals they were trying to meet in fund-raising.

The Phone Center truly had a team environment. Supervisors and fund-raisers helped one another by acknowledging good work, giving one another advice on how to handle difficult questions and refusals from alumni, and quizzing one another on university facts. The supervisors often implemented role-play situations before shifts began in order to simulate common situations that fund-raisers ran into while on the phones for a specific fund. Unless trustees (those alumni who pledge more than $2,000 per year) were in the building, the dress code was always casual in the Phone Center. It was designed to have a fun, youthful atmosphere. Students were encouraged to take time to establish rapport with alumni by inviting them to hear university speakers, participate in tours, or attend sporting events in addition to asking for their financial support.

Fund-raisers were allowed a fifteen-minute break for every four hours they worked, but the structure of the breaks was flexible. The break could be taken any time after an hour into the shift, and the fund-raisers were given the option of not taking their break if they were "on a roll on the phones." If that were the case, , they could leave fifteen minutes early at the end of their shift. If a fund-raiser were struggling in the middle of a shift, a supervisor would usually pull him or her off the phones for a break and talk about new ideas to try on the phone. Overall, the flexible timing of the breaks created a positive atmosphere for the student workers and helped them better meet their goals.

When the fund-raisers met major project goals, the supervisors would plan Phone Center events such as trips to the bowling alley, a movie night, dinner at a restaurant, or a pizza party to reward them for their hard work. On pizza party nights or for the holiday party, the Phone Center would be closed the last two hours of the shift for the celebration. Supervisors also organized weekend outings for the staff to increase morale and keep the Phone Center a fun place for students to work.

Overall, the Phone Center usually met but didn't exceed its annual goals. The goals were set in collaboration between Amelia and the executive board and were considered realistic financial targets. However, the economic downturn and decreasing endowment were making it essential for the university to acquire additional external funding. This was putting pressure on the Annual Giving Department and the Phone Center to raise their goals and bring in more alumni donations. At the same time, Amelia's job responsibilities were increasing and she found it difficult to manage all aspects of her job.

NEW STRUCTURE AND ASSISTANT DIRECTOR

In order to provide stronger oversight to the Phone Center and help it reach higher goals, Amelia and the executive board created the position of assistant director of annual giving. This decision changed the managerial design and organization structure of the Phone Center. The main duty of the new assistant director was to oversee the management of the Phone Center, thus relieving Amelia of direct supervision of the Phone Center staff. This in turn allowed her to focus on higher-level fund-raising issues.

Robert was hired as the assistant director. He was a university alum who had previously worked as a fund-raiser and a supervisor in the Phone Center before graduating. Rachel and Jesse, two of the senior student supervisors, had worked with Robert and considered him a friend. Robert had been their supervisor when they were first-year students, and they had been equals with Robert when all three were hired to supervisor positions. Rachel and Jesse were excited that the assistant director would be someone they knew and respected. They remembered Robert being relaxed, laid-back, and respectful. They also remembered that he was the first to volunteer to leave a shift if there were not enough fund-raisers signed up to warrant two supervisors on the shift. Robert did not take his job as supervisor too seriously and had just done what he needed to do to get his paycheck. He was fun to be around, but not really a strong leader. They assumed he would be the same old Robert.

According to the new structure and job description of assistant director, Robert was going to be at five of the seven weekly Phone Center calling shifts to direct the fund-raisers and the supervisors, adding another layer of management. The student supervisors, Rachel, Jesse, Christine, and Jeremy, were now to complete the regular nightly report and meet weekly with Robert instead of Amelia. Robert also would directly supervise them during a shift. This was a major change in the work environment that gave them less autonomy and discretion. The supervisors now felt that they had to look over their shoulders when Robert was on a shift. Figure 1 depicts the new structure.

It was immediately clear that Robert's leadership style was much different from Amelia's. Robert was very strict, and his number one priority was raising the most money possible on each shift. Incentives, creativity, and entertainment were far down on his list of priorities. The supervisors, on the other hand, were accustomed to creating a fun environment where employees would want to raise as much money as possible. They liked to inspire, not

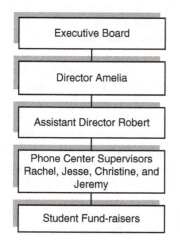

FIGURE 1 New Phone Center Organizational Structure

mandate. Robert's style clearly clashed with the Phone Center's culture and the preferences and expectations of the supervisors and fund-raisers.

CONFLICT BETWEEN RACHEL AND ROBERT

One of the supervisors, Rachel, was the most dissatisfied with Robert's leadership and management approach. Rachel was the most experienced supervisor on the team. Although they had worked together well in the past, Robert wanted nothing to do with Rachel's ideas for creative innovations. For example, Rachel had suggested splitting up the fund-raisers into mixed teams of top fund-raisers and struggling fund-raisers to compete in a "Survivor" game. Robert, however, wanted to see all the callers in their seats before the shift started, and he didn't want any of them to be out of their seats except on their breaks. Rachel's ideas for the game would not work very well in an environment in which the fund-raisers were not allowed out of their seats to celebrate pledges or to participate in a game or activity.

Rachel was disappointed that Robert was not allowing the supervisors as much freedom or creativity in decision making as they formerly had. This freedom allowed them to create motivational games, competitions, or incentives while keeping up morale so fund-raisers were excited to come to work. Before Robert came into the office, the supervisors used team games such as "The Amazing Race," Phone Center Monopoly, bingo, basketball, and "hot potato" to keep the fund-raisers excited about participation, upgrades in gifts from the last amount an alum had given, and credit card gifts. Now, Robert insisted that the supervisors should not be out of their seats to play a game after getting a pledge because that was wasting good time during which successful fund-raisers could be soliciting another pledge.

Robert also cut back on the fund-raisers' break time and was inflexible about how that time was to be used. He did not trust the fund-raisers to take their break when they felt they needed it. Instead, he insisted that every fund-raiser take his or her break at exactly 7:30, and if they were on a call at that time, then they didn't get their full ten minutes. Rachel remembered how much she needed breaks when she was a fund-raiser, and she was angry with Robert for taking five minutes away from their break and their freedom of when to take it.

Robert refused to close the Phone Center for outings as a reward for meeting project goals; he also thought that bringing in food for break time would make fund-raisers lose their focus. He wanted the Phone Center to be about business and making money. As a result, the fund-raisers didn't seem as excited about getting a pledge because the games and incentives they were used to were nearly eliminated. Rachel felt as though she was letting the fund-raisers down rather than rewarding them for their hard work and motivating them to get back on the phones. Rachel now felt that her job was not fun, exciting, or rewarding anymore, and she started dreading going to work. With the supervisors having less freedom to create fun activities in the Phone Center, morale was negatively affected across the board.

CENTRALIZED DECISION MAKING AND AUTHORITY

Robert believed that he knew what was best for the Phone Center. After all, he was now responsible for its fiscal success in fund-raising. Robert wanted to take advantage of the skills of his best fund-raisers in order to get the best statistics every night. To him, this meant they needed to work nearly every shift and stay on the phones the entire time to make the most contacts possible. The supervisors thought that Robert should also focus on what made his best fund-raisers as good as they were: skill development with help and coaching from supervisors.

Robert's method was to constantly monitor fund-raisers to ensure that they were doing their best on every single call. Robert was not afraid of using the fear of getting caught using the incorrect techniques on the phone to make certain that the fund-raisers were always acting with a view to bringing in a profit. The supervisors believed that the fund-raisers should not always be in fear of losing their job and should be able to express their own styles and try different techniques in phone conversations, connecting with alumni and positively reflecting the university. Robert thought that the fund-raisers' paychecks were the motivation for them to do well because he could always take them away by firing them. The supervisors believed that fund-raisers needed motivation that went beyond the hourly wage by involving fun, friendly competition, prizes, bonus incentives, and rewards. Robert often said, "This is one of the best-paying jobs in town for students. Isn't that enough? That should be all they need."

After about a month with the new structure in place, Rachel, Jesse, Christine, and Jeremy were informed in a weekly meeting that three new student supervisors would be hired instead of the one or two additions that were previously planned for the next semester. This brought with it the stipulation that each supervisor would now be supervising two shifts per week instead of three and would be in the role of student fund-raiser one shift per week (thus replacing one supervisor shift with one calling shift each week).

All four supervisors were shocked because Robert had not even brought up this idea before, so they had had no time to digest it. Robert made this decision without considering input from Rachel, Jesse, Christine, or Jeremy, even though they used to be equals in the organization. Rachel was especially hurt because this was her third year as a supervisor, and Amelia had always listened to her opinions and input before making a big decision like this that would affect her position. There was immediate tension in the room because the supervisors felt robbed: they had worked hard as fund-raisers and, through the interview process, advanced to supervisors so they would graduate to higher responsibilities than just the phones. Rachel asked Robert why he had made this decision, and he stated that supervisors should be some of his best fund-raisers because of their training, and the whole point of the Phone Center was to raise money. Rachel understood that fund-raising was the main reason that the Phone Center had been created, but she also knew that alumni outreach and education were equally important in gaining alumni support. She believed that Robert was interested only in money and not in the talented people who were working for the Phone Center.

With these new rules in place, the boundaries concerning interaction between supervisors and fund-raisers broke down. The lines of authority had become unclear. This was because the supervisors were in the position of being the fund-raisers' equals one shift per week and their supervisors with authority over them two shifts per week. Rachel was uneasy and nervous because she needed to prove that what she was coaching the fund-raisers to do two nights per week would bring her success also (practicing what she preached, so to speak). Moreover, because Rachel had only one night of calling statistics per week; a bad night on the phone could be detrimental to her weekly stats, which could tarnish her credibility in the eyes of the student fund-raisers she coached. Rachel felt as though she had been demoted by having to work one shift per week at a lower level in the department hierarchy than what she was hired to do. Jesse, Christine, and Jeremy told her they felt the same way, but they didn't want to stand up to Robert and risk losing their jobs or making Robert dislike them for questioning his authority.

Rachel was very unhappy in her position as supervisor, and she knew she could not hide her discontent while coaching the fund-raisers or working with fellow supervisors. She tried to leave her bad attitude at the door before she walked into the Phone Center, but she knew she just was not being as effective in doing her job as she once was. Rachel believed that her options were (a) to quit because she was no longer as respected or effective in her position; (b) go over Robert's head to Amelia and express her concerns professionally, explain her unhappiness, and see what Amelia could do to remedy the situation; or (c) try and mediate with Robert in a private meeting.

Rachel did not want to give up the job she had worked so hard at for three years, but she knew she would not be effective or happy if she stayed under these circumstances. Rachel knew that Amelia had faith in Robert and that just because his management style was different from Amelia's didn't mean that he was wrong. Rachel did not want to look like a tattletale to Amelia, and she did not want to make it look like she could not adapt to new situations. Rachel also knew that a meeting with Robert would prove to be difficult because he was set in his ways and saw her as being below him in the hierarchy. If she did choose to meet privately with Robert, she would have a difficult time keeping emotions out of the conversation. Rachel didn't know what to do.

Discussion Questions

1. What are the strengths and weaknesses of Robert's versus Amelia's leadership styles?
2. Describe the approach to motivation that appears to work best for the student fund-raisers. How does Robert's style conflict with this approach?

3. Do you think that Robert was hired to bring about change? How could Robert and Amelia have better prepared the Phone Center for the changes in leadership and culture?

4. What action steps do you suggest for Rachel? How can she balance her desire to excel at her job with her dissatisfaction with the new management style?

5. What needs to be done to improve the morale of the Phone Center staff before it's too late? How can the Annual Giving Department reach its higher goals?

THE ISLAMIC CENTER CASE

Robert A. Cropf,
Jennifer M. Giancola, and
Nauman Wadalawala

OVERVIEW

Abstract

The Islamic Center is a nonprofit organization with a small staff that relies heavily on volunteers from the Muslim community. This case study examines the conflicts that arise as a result of environmental changes that lead to increased tensions that threaten the organization's core mission and its central place in the community. The changes in question include increased size and membership, which lead to tensions about how the center should expand. The actual day-to-day administration of the facility is also affected by these changes, resulting in conflicts and leading to loss of morale and other leadership problems.

Main Topics

Implementation, Planning

Secondary Topics

Human resources administration, Leadership

Teaching Purpose

To discuss how a nonprofit community organization can respond effectively to tensions created by dramatic changes in its environment.

The Organization

An Islamic center in a midsized city in the Western part of the United States with a small but growing Muslim population

Main Characters

- Ahmed Kader, Founder and Board Member
- Abdel Rahman, Gymnasium Staff Member
- The Board of the Islamic Center

BACKGROUND

In 1965, the Muslim community in an urban area of a Western state was very small—mostly foreign students at the local university and some of their family members. Although they were few in number, these individuals formed a chapter of the national organization, the Muslim Student Association (MSA), at the university. The chapter grew tremendously in the subsequent years. The transition from a fledgling club to an award-winning organization took time and effort, especially since MSA was the only organization supporting the local Muslim community in the region. In the beginning, MSA membership was low and members met for prayers and other activities at the facilities provided by the university. Eventually, as the Muslim community in the area started to grow, the membership of the MSA increased and the association moved its prayers and meetings to a nearby international center.

After years of being active in the MSA, several alumni believed that if they were going to stay in the city, they should form an organization independent of the university. Ahmed Kader, a former president of the MSA, and a number of his peers formed the Islamic Center (IC), a nonprofit organization that served as a haven for Muslims in the region. Ahmed, who had become a civil engineer and had many contacts, helped the IC purchase an old office building from the Jones Construction Company and, after holding a number of fund-raising events, enough funds were collected to fix the office building and turn it into a community center.

THE NEXT STEP: A NEW HOME

As time passed, Ahmed and the leadership of the IC realized that with the continued growth of the Muslim community in the area, an even larger facility was needed. In 1987, Ahmed led negotiations that allowed the organization to purchase a five-acre plot of land in a suburban area. Fund-raising proved useful again in procuring enough money to construct a new building that would house a larger mosque. On November 27, 1992, a groundbreaking ceremony was held; the mosque officially opened to the public in November 1995. Having been built from scratch, it looked more like a traditional mosque than a converted office building. It featured traditional elements such as a dome-shaped ceiling, pillars, and a minaret. The Daar-Ul-Islam (The House of Islam) was the official name of the new mosque, which quickly became the center of the regional Muslim community.

In the years since it was built, Daar-Ul-Islam has developed the largest membership of any mosque in the state. There is a full-time elementary school at the mosque with approximately 200 students in attendance, and every Friday, about 600 people attend the congregational prayer called Jum'ah. The mosque also hosts an Arabic school on Saturdays with 100 students and a Sunday school that has about 300 students each week. The busiest times at the mosque are during the two major holidays in Islam. The first is Eid-al-Fitr, which is a celebration that occurs at the end of fasting during the month of

Ramadan. The second holiday is Eid-al-Adha, which is a festival of sacrifice that occurs during the time when Muslims make a pilgrimage to Makkah. Both of these holidays draw up to 3,000 people to the mosque for prayers.

The Islamic Center is operated as a nonprofit organization with a staff that relies heavily on volunteers from the community. Currently the foundation employs two spiritual leaders, three full-time secretaries, and two janitorial service teams. In addition, there are an estimated 100 teachers, staff, and volunteers for all the different schools at the mosque.

THE ROLE OF THE BOARD OF DIRECTORS

The Board of Directors, also known as the Majlis Shura, is the primary decision-making group of the IC. The board consists of fifteen elected individuals. Of the fifteen members, four comprise the executive committee. The executive committee consists of a chair, vice chair, treasurer, and general secretary. Each of the terms for these officials is three years long. Also, five board members are retired and replaced by new board members every year. The constitution of the IC clearly states that the Board of Directors is solely responsible for approval or disapproval of most of the decisions that need to be made in the IC. This is true of any expansion or construction projects involving the IC building, which makes the board an integral player in the proposed construction of a gymnasium facility at the IC.

The first question the Board of Directors asked when deciding what kind of facility to build was, "What are our priorities?" The second question was, "What is the purpose of the building?" There were different perspectives in response to these questions. The first was that the gymnasium would be built solely for the elementary school and that the gym would fall under the administration of the school. This was not unusual: in fact many schools have gymnasiums as a part of their facilities. These schools also open their gyms to the general public so that they may be reserved for private events. Many years ago, the IC held its Eid congregations at a similar facility other than the mosque, because it could not accommodate the large number of people who came to pray. One such school gymnasium at a nearby high school was used to hold the Eid congregation of 3,000 people. The IC simply had to reserve the gym from the high school's administration.

The leaders of the IC had to determine if they wanted a similar purpose for the gymnasium at Daar-Ul-Islam. Taking this route would add school stakeholders to the planning and execution process of building the gym. The school administration would also have the final say as to which events were to be held in the gym. By doing this, the school would be allowed to make decisions with its own interest in mind. However, building the gym as part of the school would put the administrative responsibilities in the hands of the school and not the community at large.

Another route for the IC was to build a gymnasium solely as a business enterprise. The purpose of the gym then would be both to generate enough revenue to cover the costs of building and to create some income for the IC.

If this were to be the case, the gymnasium would need to be independent of the school and would require a separate management staff. As a business, the IC would attempt to encourage as many of the community members as possible to join the gym as a way of guaranteeing its success. Members could use the gym on an individual basis or come to play volleyball, badminton, and basketball against other members. Also, the gymnasium would be used as a hall for private parties and events. Renting out the gym to the public would generate profits in addition to the membership fees. If this course were taken, then the school would be using the community's building, but the school administration would not be making the decisions—the gym administration would.

These two alternative purposes of the gymnasium led to the second, important, question, "How was the building to be used?" This question helped determine not only the day-to-day management of the facility, but also the long-term major priorities of the IC. In terms of facility administration, there were three issues that needed to be addressed: space allocation, cost allocation, and staff allocation.

If the gymnasium were used for the school, then the building's space would be allocated according to the school's best interest. For cost allocation, the school would have to work out a new budget in which the gym was included. This would result in an increase in tuition for the students because the school would be responsible for maintaining the building. However, the benefits for students would include better facilities and the addition of new programs such as gym classes and after-school programs. For staff allocation, the school would definitely have to add new members to the current staff in order to administer the gym: a physical education staff, after-school activities coordinator, evening manager, and weekend manager would all be necessary.

If the gymnasium were used as a community center, then a new set of concerns for the administration of the building would arise. With regard to space allocation, the gym would be used to support a full-fledged community center, one that provided community members with the services they desired. The hours of operation would need to be scheduled with the community's convenience in mind. For cost allocation, the IC would have to add the budget of the new gym to its current operating fund, which was already near deficit levels. Finally, regarding staff allocation, the IC would employ a director to oversee staff and to manage the responsibilities associated with the gym. The gym would also serve as a community center, and, hence, the staff would have responsibilities for managing both the gymnasium and community center aspects of the facility.

The board of the IC determined that the answers to both questions required diagramming and discussing all possible solutions. Several on the board thought that the gymnasium needed to be an income-generating facility and community center. Still others wanted the school to be the top priority, with the gym as a secondary one. Their concerns were heightened when funds were raised to build the gym portion of the new building before funds were raised to add more classrooms to the school. The mosque extension project continued on to the classrooms when enough resources could be collected to build them.

One member of the fund-raising committee asked, "Why is it that the gym was built first and then the school, logically speaking, shouldn't the school come first?"

The answer several board members gave was, "Once the gym is up and running, then the entire community will start seeing that we're serious about completing the work that needs to be done. When the community members see the gym project completed and successful, they will donate accordingly because they'll see that the IC means business."

Promises were also made to donors about how the opening of the gym would generate more involvement of the younger generation in the IC. Parents thought that the gym would help get the younger generation more involved with the mosque. The youth of the community were involved with non-Muslim school activities, friends, and other recreational activities, and the IC wanted these children to start becoming active members of the Muslim community. The idea was that because most kids loved playing sports, the gym would be a good way to attract young people to the mosque and, once there, get them more involved in the community.

A number of people from the IC had strong opinions about the subject. The chair of the Board of Directors, two board members, and the chair of the gymnasium committee all met and discussed major questions to assess whether or not the gym project had turned out as planned. They tried to determine what the plans were before the gym was built; they wanted to see if the community's ideal plan for the gym ever existed.

One individual said, "The master plans for the gym were made back in 1989 and the ideal plan was for the gym to be used by the entire community." Another man said, "There were quite a few superb plans for the gym during the design phase, but unfortunately, due to the lack of funding and leadership, many of the plans had to be abandoned. The ideal plan of the gym was to provide a safer environment for our younger generation; to cater to the needs of the school; to make the facility available for men, women, and children of the community for working out and indoor sports; and to be able to rent the gym for various sporting occasions and community events."

Whether or not the project plans were executed according to the community's exact desire, the gymnasium was built. Left undecided, however, was the facility's main purpose.

THE OPENING OF THE GYMNASIUM

After the opening of the gym, the excitement over the new facility was apparent and everyone wanted to get involved. The gym staff members were thrilled to be a part of the project because not only was the workload light, but they would be paid for the hours they put in (a nice change from volunteer work). The gymnasium staff consisted of a supervisor, assistant, and staff consisting of community youth selected through an application process. Among them was Abdel Rahman, a young man who had previously volunteered at the mosque. Abdel's father served on the current Board of

Directors of the IC and was the chair during a brief period in the 1990s. Upon being hired, staff members were informed that they would serve as gym staff only temporarily until full-time adult staff could be hired. Because Abdel and the other teenagers were in school, there was no way to schedule gym staff for more than a part-time position.

Abdel's duties at the gymnasium were fairly simple. He was paid on an hourly basis, and he had to be at the gym at least a half hour before his scheduled shift. The entire gym court needed to be swept and cleaned. Toward the end of the day, Abdel and the other staff had to make sure the gym was clean: the basketball backboards had to be washed, the wall and column pads had to be cleaned, and the bathrooms had to be sanitary and orderly.

Another one of Abdel's responsibilities was to work the reception desk. The reception desk at the gym needed to be set up daily. At the reception table, Abdel was responsible for making sure that each person who entered the gym signed in. The patron then decided which type of membership he or she would like to purchase: daily membership ($2 for one day), weekly membership ($5 for one week), or monthly membership ($25 for one month). When the gymnasium first opened, the committee set the hours of operation as: Monday through Thursday, 5 p.m. to 10 p.m., Friday and Saturday from 6 p.m. to 12:00 a.m., and Sunday from 12:00 p.m. until 3:00 p.m. From the beginning, attendance was high, especially relative to the number of people in the community. There were around thirty-five people every Monday and Wednesday, a combination of both adults and youth. Mondays and Wednesdays about twenty adults would come to play badminton and/or volleyball, and then ten to fifteen youth would come to play basketball. Friday nights were the busiest nights, with attendance around fifty to sixty people coming to play basketball over the course of the evening.

BUILDING A MUSLIM COMMUNITY

Social capital refers to the trust and relationships that bring and keep community members together, allowing them to achieve their common goals more effectively. The people who participate in the gym all have common goals, as do the members of the IC board. The gym participants are there to exercise, to play sports, and to have an enjoyable time. People of all age groups attend the gym to play badminton, volleyball, or basketball. When he was not working, Abdel would often go to the gym to play badminton or volleyball with the adults. They would talk about upcoming community events and politics. By having conversations with these adults, Abdel formed a bond with them that extended beyond the gym. Another good thing about the gym was that it allowed people to get to know one another on a personal level. For example, after playing basketball Friday nights, all of the players would go to dinner together. This allowed Abdel and others to meet new people and widen their social circles.

The IC board members want to strengthen the Muslim community in the area. They recognize that this can be done by increasing the social connections and ties among the area's Muslims. On the one hand, some of this occurs naturally as the result of being a religious minority in a predominantly Christian society. However, as noted previously, the community's adults are concerned that distractions are diverting the youth away from community activities, which could mean that the social bonds connecting future generations of Muslims in the area may become looser and result in a less cohesive community, at least from the perspective of the current generation of adults. Another concern has to do with the fragmentation of the Muslim community into several subgroups, each with its own competing interests.

For many Muslims, another advantage of the facility was that it encouraged unity among the different ethnic groups in the area. Bosnians, African Americans, Indians, Pakistanis, and Arabs would all come together to participate in sports and exercise at the gym. These people formed long-term friendships despite their linguistic and cultural differences. This, in turn, helped unify the different groups and broaden the diversity of the mosque and the Muslim community as a whole.

Nevertheless, not all social bonds of this sort result in positive outcomes. There are also negative characteristics of strong social connections, which include intense pressures toward exclusion and conformity and social and economic class pressures. These effects can become destructive within a tight-knit community. Although the gym did not spawn gangs, some other negative aspects of close social ties did emerge. For example, Abdel noticed that people who felt the same way about mosque politics began to form cliques. Each group worked hard to recruit members and promote its own agenda. As a teenager, Abdel was not very interested in the politics and infighting in his community; he believed that everyone should try to work for common goals.

Conformity-enhancing effects are the result of intense pressure for social conformity that often accompanies tight-knit communities such as faith-based organizations. This was a problem frequently observed at the facility. Unfortunately, because the same people come to the gymnasium every week, the norms and behaviors of some of the attendees tended to rub off on the others. For example, if one young person had expensive basketball shoes, others began to want the same thing, which created divisions and encouraged overly materialistic behaviors. Exclusionary effects can result from strong group ties that can act as obstacles to outsiders who want to participate in a community. Abdel loved the gym because it was a place where these effects were noticeably absent. For example, when he first started attending the gym, Abdel was welcomed by the adults to play volleyball and badminton with them, even though he was clearly much younger. Another example was the few non-Muslims who came to the gymnasium to play basketball on Friday nights. It would have been easy for people to not let them play. However, the non-Muslim players were treated with the same respect and kindness as everyone else.

Arguably, the gymnasium has helped build more of the positive social ties. The gym promoted closeness among the different groups and supported diversity and other positive attributes, which had an overall positive effect for the area's Muslim community. Consequently, it has become an integral part of the IC and has helped boost the organization's credibility among the community's young people.

A TURN FOR THE WORSE

After a year of good attendance at the gymnasium, things began to slowly change. First, the gymnasium staff began to turn over with great rapidity. The director was the first to leave because he felt that he did not have the resources to properly manage the facility. After his departure, three other staff members quickly followed. These people were doing the job only as a favor to the director, and since he was gone that meant they were free of their obligation. Several other individuals resigned because of school or because they moved away from the area. Abdel decided to stay, along with one other coworker. The two of them realized that their responsibilities were soon going to increase considerably. They decided to work two days a week each and alternate every other Friday. Abel stayed on the staff with the expectation that the Board of Directors would hire more people because it was very difficult for two people to take on the workload of many individuals. As time passed, however, nobody was hired. Instead, the IC decided to operate the facility with part-time volunteers in addition to the decimated full-time staff. Eventually, the workload became too much for Abdel to handle, and the hours of operation at the gym had to be cut significantly. Even with abbreviated hours, however, Abdel eventually felt he had to leave his job because it became too difficult.

For a period of three weeks, the gymnasium was completely closed due to a lack of gym staff, which led to a sharp decline in community usage. People began to go to other gyms.

Ultimately, the Board of Directors asked Abdel, despite his youth, to step in as a part-time director to run the gymnasium. He found some volunteers who were willing to help operate the gym on Wednesdays, Fridays, and Sundays. The hours of operation were still not the same as before the three-week shutdown, but it was better than not being open at all. This may have solved some problems temporarily and seemed like a great plan; however, in the long run, this was not going to work. It was important to have more than just one full-time employee responsible for operating the entire facility.

The decline of the gym was beginning to harm the area's entire Muslim community. Rather than the gymnasium being used to encourage greater social interactions and for the strengthening of social bonds, the lack of personnel was curtailing people's use of the facility, and the facility was not being used to its capacity. Also, the lack of consistent hours and staff professionalism resulted in much frustration, leading, in some instances, to cases of vandalism.

During Abdel's time as part-time gymnasium director, he had to solve several issues. Some of these were anticipated incidents, and they were addressed in the monthly meetings with the entire staff. Because of the preparation, the staff had a plan to handle the issues. Some situations the staff would have to deal with on a continuing basis. For example, children would come to the gym and insist that their parents would pay their membership fee at a later date. Many of them got a free ride because those fees were never paid. Also, arguments would arise among the patrons of the gym. In addition, people would break into the gym after the hours of operation. At other times, the problem was that patrons did not follow the rules of the gym, such as no food allowed. They thought that if they were paying, they should be able to do what they wanted. The last problem was that there was not always one identifiable person in charge. This would result in the heating or cooling system being left running, the lights left on, or the doors left unlocked after gym hours.

THE BACKLASH: A VANDALISM INCIDENT

On a Friday in November, an incident of vandalism occurred after a conflict over the operation of the gymnasium. The scheduled hours of operation for that day were 6:00 p.m. to 10:00 p.m. A group of thirty to forty people went to the gym assuming that it was open. When they arrived, however, the gym was locked and all the lights were turned off. One of the patrons had Abdel's number and asked him to come to the gym and open it up for everyone to play. The director came down as soon as possible. Upon his arrival, he noticed that there were tables and chairs set up on the basketball court. He made a few phone calls and was told by the gymnasium committee chair that a dinner was to be held in the gymnasium the next day. Nobody was allowed to enter the gym for the night. When the people heard this news, they were frustrated at being turned away. A majority of them simply went home or found some place else to play. However, some ten to fifteen people began to vandalize the gym and damage Abdel's car. This incident brought home to the board that the gym, far from being a uniting element in the community, was turning into a divisive factor and that something needed to be done to face this issue.

LEADERSHIP TROUBLES

The ad hoc gymnasium committee was formed in January 2008 as a response to the vandalism incident. The constitution of the IC did not include the gymnasium committee because the gym was relatively new. However, there were references to the responsibilities of committees in general. For example, it said in the constitution that, "each committee shall meet once a month, or as determined by its Chairperson." Because the guidelines are very general, the gym committee did not feel pressured to meet often. It also did not have a set agenda to follow. The committee could not actually make major decisions; it could only recommend policies to the board. The Majlis Shura then made the decision on whether or not the advice of the committee should be implemented.

The committee determined that the administration of the gymnasium was too loose. The board provided little or no direction to the gym staff. There was no financial benefit in being on the Board of Directors or a committee; the people were truly doing the work because of their religious dedication and love for their community. The individuals in these leadership positions wanted to do what was best for the community. It is important to recognize the central role that leaders have in the Muslim community. They are typically the most successful members of the community and are generally looked upon with a great deal of respect. The gym had great potential to strengthen the area's Muslim community, but, in part, because of poor leadership, it seems to be producing more harm than good.

Another factor that played a part in the gym situation was lack of motivation. All the leaders of the IC, other than the two spiritual leaders, were volunteers. Thus, there were very few incentives, other than nonmaterial ones, to serve as motivators for the gym staff. Fortunately, the community was blessed with numerous professionals such as doctors, engineers, lawyers, and accountants who served in leadership roles. These were usually volunteers who were doing this work for intrinsic rewards and that is what kept them motivated. Since material gain cannot serve as the motivating factor for people in the mosque community, the solution to the problem must lay, in part, with the internal desire to serve the community and gain spiritual rewards. With the hard work of the leaders, the gym may be able to become an important community resource.

Discussion Questions

1. Imagine yourself an IC board member. You have financial obligations on one hand, but on the other hand you have an obligation to the community. How do you strike a balance between the two objectives such that you help your community grow and remain close while also watching the bottom line?

2. What steps would you take as a member of the ad hoc committee to make the gym a better facility for everyone? How would you implement those changes?

3. How would you incentivize members of the community, both young and old, to contribute time to the gym, recognizing the distractions many people face?

4. How should the building be primarily used: as a community center or a sports facility? How could the facility be used most effectively to strengthen the community's social ties?

5. Given the community's constraints, how can the IC cultivate new leadership styles, especially among the youth?

10 | READNOW!

Robert A. Cropf,
Jennifer M. Giancola, and
Cassandra Slattery

OVERVIEW

Abstract

In this case, a local chapter of a national nonprofit organization continuously struggles with funding and must, therefore, be proactive in seeking out additional revenue sources. The local coordinator encounters a situation involving a potential donor that forces her to weigh the pros and cons of breaking the rules and the best way to communicate her concerns to her superiors and the donor. A chance meeting on a flight leads to a potential conflict-of-interest situation for the local coordinator.

Main Topics

Decision making, Ethics

Secondary Topics

Communication, Intergovernmental affairs*

Teaching Purpose

To discuss the complexities involved in balancing personal and organizational responsibilities within the framework of a nonprofit organization.

The Organization

ReadNow is a nonprofit program that promotes early literacy by giving new books to children and advice to parents about the importance of reading aloud in pediatric exam rooms across the nation.*

---

* Relations between central headquarters and a local organization.

Main Characters:
- Michael Vaughn, Executive Vice President of Johnson Hospital
- Dr. Lea Nelson, Head of National ReadNow
- Patricia Clay, Local ReadNow Coordinator
- Molly Carter, Tillingast Foundation employee
- Dr. Katie Nelson, ReadNow Local Director

BACKGROUND

In 1962, a group of doctors at a hospital in Phoenix, Arizona, were brainstorming ways to increase early childhood literacy and parent–child interactions among their patients. One doctor had the idea of distributing children's books to their patients during checkups, accompanied by advice to the parents about the importance of reading aloud to their children. From this modest beginning, ReadNow developed into a national, nonprofit organization that distributes books and early literacy guidance to more than 2.5 million children and their families. ReadNow has offices all over the United States and is currently supported in part through a grant from the U.S. Department of Education.

ReadNow opened a branch in Crown City, Michigan, in August with a partnership between the National ReadNow and the Johnson Children's Medical Center. One of the founders, Dr. Mark Jeffries, still active within ReadNow, approached Dr. Katie Nelson, a pediatrician at Johnson Hospital with the opportunity to bring ReadNow to Crown City. Dr. Nelson soon had more than thirty pediatric clinics participating in the program and hired a coordinator, Patricia Clay, to manage the day-to-day operations of the Crown City chapter.

As a result of its affiliation with the Johnson Children's Medical Center, ReadNow was fortunate to have its rent, computers, telephones, and office supplies provided by the hospital. Johnson Children's Medical Center agreed to support the office environment of ReadNow, as well as to guarantee the coordinator a stipend of $50,000 each year. However, part of Patricia Clay's duties included raising funds to purchase books to distribute in clinics across the metropolitan area and to pay for a small staff. The annual book budget for 2010 was $74,932, which needed to be raised entirely by private donations and grants from corporations and community foundations. The personnel budget for ReadNow was $65,000, which was used to pay for two staff members, an administrative assistant and a secretary. Additionally, the organization relied on volunteers, who were recruited around the area at events that required some funds to plan and execute. Throughout the year, parties were held for the volunteers to build team spirit. Workshops, retreats, and training seminars also were held for staff and volunteers. The total expense of these events in 2010 was $50,000. Therefore, the coordinator was responsible for raising nearly $190,000 a year mainly through contributions.

The Johnson Children's Medical Center put one severe restriction on Patricia's fund-raising efforts. Johnson Hospital, a nonprofit itself, relied heavily on support from the community to support its operations. Therefore, the hospital strongly discouraged Patricia from soliciting funds from any organization or individual already contributing money to the hospital. This was done to avoid "double dipping" in fund-raising, since ReadNow was associated with the Johnson Children's Medical Center, and the center committed itself to major support of the nonprofit. The hospital's management thought that for ReadNow to ask money from the same corporations or foundations might significantly undercut the center's own fund-raising efforts.

The rationale for the opposition to more than one contribution per donor developed out of an awkward situation that Michael Vaughn, executive vice president of Johnson Hospital, encountered when he first began working for the hospital. At that time, Johnson Children's Medial Center supported a smoking cessation program, Hugs Not Ashes (HNA), which operated out of the asthma clinic at the hospital. The leaders of that program did not have the same restrictions placed on its fund-raising and were free to solicit funds from whomever they chose. Unfortunately, they wrote a fund-raising proposal to one of Crown City's most wealthy and well-known donors, Elizabeth Jones, who was on the board of the Johnson Foundation. When she received numerous letters from the coordinator of HNA, she became so offended that she was being solicited twice for donations that she recanted her support for Johnson Hospital and became a large funder of Anderson Hospital, the other pediatric medical facility in Crown City. The loss of Jones's support, accompanied by the embarrassment the coordinator of HNA caused, resulted in the cancellation of the program and the resulting limitations on fund-raising for ReadNow.

The local ReadNow's support consists of a joint effort of federal funding (25 percent), foundation grants (10 percent), private donations (50 percent), and support from the Johnson Foundation (15 percent). The national center of ReadNow secures roughly 10 percent of federal funding for state and city coalitions, of which the metropolitan area of Crown City is a member. The remaining 75 percent of funding is up to the coordinators to raise from corporations, grants, and individuals. The Johnson Foundation stresses the importance of the coalition's seeking its own funding because of its large need of funds and the projects it supports.

As a result of its affiliation with the hospital, the chapter's organizational culture is more closely tied to the fortunes of Johnson than to its own national office. This has both positive and negative ramifications for the daily operations of the Crown City ReadNow chapter. On the plus side of the ledger, the chapter feels truly a part of the Johnson Medical Center and is given support for its endeavors. On the minus side, however, the chapter must abide by different guidelines than those that govern typical ReadNow chapters elsewhere. The national office firmly believes in a decentralized approach and, although its fund-raising rules are far less restrictive than the hospital's, it will not impose them on the local chapter.

PATRICIA CLAY AND MOLLY CARTER

Patricia Clay, the ReadNow coordinator, works very hard to secure funding to purchase books and to support the other activities of ReadNow. During her first month on the job, she submitted a list of more than fifty possible grants and corporations she wanted to solicit for funds. However, Emily Richards, Michael Vaughn's assistant at Johnson Hospital, told her that there already was a relationship with most of the funders on her list and narrowed her possibilities down to seven family foundations to apply to for a grant. There was no corporation included on Emily's list. Undaunted, Patricia began networking with community groups to try to get support for the program.

Within a few months, Patricia developed a plan to have local community groups "adopt" a pediatric clinic participating in the ReadNow program. The group would donate enough money for that particular clinic's book budget, generally between $1,000 and $2,000. By breaking the budget down into manageable segments, Patricia ensured that clinics could afford to purchase enough books for the clinics. She was also able to increase private contributions. However, there still was a significant fund-raising gap for the staff and volunteer expenses. Patricia approached the end of the year with a budget shortfall of nearly $35,000. These funds needed to be raised somewhere, particularly since the holiday season was approaching, always a busy time of year for clinics because of colds and the flu. She took out the master list of foundations that the Johnson Hospital would not let her apply to and sighed in frustration. Any one of these foundations could easily grant her the $35,000 she needed. She also knew of several corporations that were willing to make contributions to ReadNow, but she was unwilling to risk alienating the hospital's officers. She knew the importance of keeping her financial backers happy. To apply to one of these foundations without permission not only could result in offending the staff at the hospital, but also could cause her to lose her job. She also was frustrated that the old-fashioned attitudes of the hospital's officers restricted her ability to make connections within the corporate community. These things weighed on her mind as she prepared to spend a weekend in Chicago with her sister, Dora.

During the short plane ride to Chicago, Patricia sat next to a pleasant-looking woman. They struck up a conversation about the hassles of travel, the new security restrictions, and their mutual difficulties with fitting all of their liquids into a quart-sized plastic bag to get through security. Finally, their conversation turned to what they both did for a living. Patricia explained her job as coordinator for ReadNow, and the challenges of fund-raising for a public service organization. The $35,000 shortfall weighing heavily on her mind, she was grateful to have a sympathetic ear to listen to her dilemma. The woman next to her listened patiently, nodding her head sympathetically as Patricia discussed the limitations the hospital imposed on her.

"Well, I certainly can understand your frustration," responded the woman. "Maybe I can do something to help. My name is Molly Carter and

I work for the Tillinghast Foundation. We're always on the lookout for new projects to fund, and we wouldn't have a problem with the amount of money you're looking to raise. Why don't you submit a proposal to me in the next few weeks, in time for our board meeting at the end of the month?"

Patricia was excited by the possibility that she might have solved ReadNow's financial problem during a brief plane ride. She took Molly's business card and promised to put together a proposal soon. As they disembarked the plane, both wished each other a pleasant weekend and went their separate ways.

Back in the office on Monday, Patricia worked furiously to write an impressive proposal for Molly and the Tillinghast Foundation's board. Looking at the foundation's income tax returns, she discovered that the board distributed significant amounts of money, upwards of $75,000! She didn't even need half that amount; in her mind, as she sat preparing the proposal, the $35,000 looked all but guaranteed. By Wednesday afternoon, Patricia had all of the necessary documents together and her annual budget prepared, and just needed the director, Dr. Katie Jones, to sign off on it.

"Looks great!" Dr. Jones exclaimed as she walked into Patricia's office with the proposal. "Did Michael give it the OK? I'm pretty sure the Tillinghast has given a grant to the center. Check with him first, then you've got my OK."

Dr. Jones turned and walked out of the room.

Patricia's face blanched as she realized she never checked to see if Tillinghast was on the list of major donors. Pulling up the list on her computer, her heart sank as she saw the foundation on it. Emily told her that the Tillinghast Foundation already gave money to the Johnson Hospital—but several years ago. Nevertheless, it was still on the list. She hesitated as she considered what to do next.

After a few minutes of deliberation, she decided to pull Molly's business card from her Rolodex to dial her number to explain the situation. Maybe Molly could help her in some way.

"What does it matter?" asked Molly making the case that (1) the foundation's giving occurred several years ago and (2) the foundation contributed to the hospital and not ReadNow. "Why don't you go ahead and submit your proposal. I really think that you have a great program that fits within the goals of the foundation. If the board agrees with me, you can just explain the situation to Michael. I'm sure he'll understand. This is an opportunity for you to fulfill your budget requirements, and for me to bring a great organization to the attention of our board members. We have a lot of contacts within the community, and I would hate to see you miss out on this prospect for funding."

Patricia hung up the phone, completely torn about what to do. On the one hand, here was a possible funder who was incredibly positive about the opportunity to get a significant amount of money for ReadNow. She had to raise $35,000 by the end of the fiscal year, which was rapidly approaching. She did not have any immediate prospects on the horizon, nor did she develop any other solution for raising the money. Patricia knew if she did not submit the proposal, she would have to work incredibly hard to try to come up with the remaining budget funds, or risk finishing the year in the red.

Furthermore, not only would she lose out on getting a big chunk of her budget funded if she passed on submitting the proposal, Patricia would also risk severing the connection she had made with Molly. She would feel awkward about approaching her in the future given her apparent mishandling of this situation. Furthermore, the points Molly made seemed to make sense to her. Particularly galling to Patricia was the apparently paternalistic attitude of the hospital's management toward ReadNow. ReadNow was a totally separate organization, yet the hospital officials thought that they could dictate to her who she could and could not contact simply because the hospital helped finance her operations. The policy against solicitation was not written down anywhere, and she had no knowledge if it had ever been enforced in the past.

On the other hand, however, she had specific instructions from Michael not to solicit funds from organizations that had supported Johnson Hospital in the past. The Tillinghast Foundation was on the list that Emily had given her detailing to whom she could not submit proposals. If she went ahead and submitted the proposal anyway, she risked the displeasure not only of Michael and Emily, but of Dr. Jones as well. She knew it was a fine line—if she were awarded the grant, most likely her boss would support her because of the amount of money she raised through one proposal. However, she thought their relationship built on trust would probably suffer as a result. Michael would most likely believe that she should have talked with him as soon as she had the conversation with Molly. If she did not receive the grant and her boss found out, she would risk reprimand for circumventing the agreement between ReadNow and the Johnson Hospital, possibly losing her job in the process. Since Patricia was still relatively new at her position, she did not want to cause conflict or confusion during her first few months on the job. The people she was in danger of crossing held a lot of influence not only as her present employer, but in the city and profession as well. These were the same people she would have to work with on upcoming projects. Would crossing them now jeopardize her employment and, possibly, future employability?

Patricia debated her options and many questions swirled around inside her head. What responsibilities did she have to foster development for ReadNow within the foundation and corporate community? What responsibilities did she have to Johnson Hospital, her primary fiscal backer? Was the chance at a great deal of money worth the risk of going against the instructions of her boss and her supporters at Johnson Hospital? Should she have communicated with her superiors sooner? Would she be crossing an ethical line by seeking funding through such a source? She carefully assembled the proposal and addressed the manila envelope to Molly at the Tillinghast Foundation. As she walked down the hall toward the mailroom, she kept debating her options, unable to decide whether or not to drop the envelope into the mail slot or into the trash can next to it.

Discussion Questions

1. What responsibilities, ethical and organizational, does Patricia have to the Johnson Medical Center? Explain.

2. How might Patricia enlist the national organization in her efforts to change the hospital's position? Explain.

3. How should Patricia have communicated her contact with Tillinghast to her superiors? Explain.

4. What would you have done if placed in this scenario? Why?

5. How might your decision affect the organization's image and networking within the community? Explain.

11 OAKDALE ADMINISTRATOR CASE

Robert A. Cropf,
Jennifer M. Giancola, and
Coley Lewis

OVERVIEW

Abstract

This case examines the political trade-offs and tough decisions that must be made to restore a municipal government to fiscal stability. In an era of flat revenue growth or decline, many municipalities face stark choices regarding economic development and growth. Oakdale, a suburb of a medium-sized city, is struggling to compete with the more prosperous and attractive surrounding municipalities for redevelopment projects and business investment. Complicating the situation is a scandal involving the previous city administrator who was found guilty of violating state ethics laws and gross fiscal malfeasance.

Main Topics

Decision making, Financial management

Secondary Topics

Political context, Ethics

Teaching Purpose

To put students in the shoes of municipal officials as they struggle to balance the budget and at the same time provide their residents with a higher quality of life.

The Organization

A small suburban municipal government with a weak economic base in the inner suburbs of a large city.

BACKGROUND

The history of Oakdale dates back to the early nineteenth century and to territories originally occupied by French and Spanish traders. There have been human settlements in the area since that time. In 1941, Oakdale officially became a state-chartered municipality and in the process established its current city government structure, creating the positions of mayor and board of aldermen and building a city hall. The current organizational chart for the City of Oakdale can be viewed in Appendix A.

Oakdale currently has a population of about 5,000 citizens according to the most recent census. The majority of Oakdale citizens are considered lower middle class, with a median income of $47,869 and a median house value of $100,900. The majority of the residents (65 percent) are white. However, a significant percentage (29 percent) is African American. The rest of the city's population consists of Native Americans and Hispanics.

Among the surrounding municipalities, Oakdale is considered something of an eyesore. So much so that citizens on the dividing line between Silver Lake City and Oakdale consider themselves residents of Silver Lake City, and even go so far as to claim that city as their mailing address. Their reasons for disavowing Oakdale are varied, but chief among them are the city's worn-out central business district and drab-looking neighborhoods. The illusion has so far worked; postal employees deliver the incorrectly labeled envelopes to those who wish to be considered residents of Silver Lake City.

Although image cannot determine the true value of a community, certain neighborhoods do appear worn, even, in some cases, seriously dilapidated. The architectural design of many retail shops and commercial establishments is outdated. Although some remodeling has been completed, along with the construction of a few new buildings, the city's business district lacks overall design consistency. Whether in a residential neighborhood or off the main artery in Oakdale, one retail store or home may look appealing and up to date; then next door, there will be another one in serious need of repair. As a result, the city appears in economic decline, which serves as a serious impediment to attracting new residents or businesses that might invest in the community. According to the city's auditors, the budget of Oakdale in 2008 was approximately $3.5 million, essentially the same as the year before. Compared to similar-sized municipalities in the same state, Oakdale lags behind in terms of

Chapter 11 • Oakdale Administrator Case

both revenues and expenditures. Therefore, city government has little in the way of available money for new projects. Without a change in the city's business climate, Oakdale's revenues and expenditures will likely decline. For instance, Silver Lake City, Oakdale's neighbor, has a population of just over 7,000, but its median income is $109,345 and the median house value is $359,888—both figures significantly greater than Oakdale's. Silver Lake City also has a higher percentage of white residents than Oakdale with 89 percent of the population being white. Silver Lake City's municipal budget is $6.7 million and has shown slight increases every year.

In April 2003, Ernie Hoffnagel, a former alderman, was elected mayor of Oakdale over the incumbent, Carl Bean. Hoffnagel, a slight man in his late fifties and a car salesman by profession, focused his campaign on revitalizing the city by attracting new businesses and residents. About a month before the election, on March 12, 2005, the local Oakdale newspaper published an interview it had recently conducted with Hoffnagel, in which he stated the following:

> This city has been in the shadows of neighboring municipalities for too long. It's time that Oakdale creates a new identity for itself. It needs a new brand: something jazzy. Too many houses and businesses are unkempt and just plain decrepit. As mayor, I'll enforce the codes; we'll have more rigorous housing inspections and see to it that our retail centers are remodeled, catching the eyes of nonresidents. I want each and every visitor to leave saying, "Wow, Oakdale is one neat place!"

Oakdale voters were immediately taken with the diminutive Hoffnagel's enthusiasm. Incumbent Carl Bean, a certified public accountant, who was more analytical than charismatic, asserted that Hoffnagel's claims were too idealistic and not fiscally feasible. Whereas Hoffnagel talked change and improvements, Bean worried over costs and budgets. Ever the politician, Hoffnagel used Bean's cautious conservatism to his advantage, contending that his opponent had not only failed to bring in new business but had not done enough as mayor to raise the city's reputation. Bean countered by enumerating all his successes during his term. However, it had little impact among the voters; the improvements, for example, fixing sidewalks here and repaving roads there, seemed relatively slight in comparison to the city's mounting image problems. The voters overwhelmingly supported the salesman, Hoffnagel, who promised a rosy future for Oakdale.

REDEVELOPING OAKDALE

With his victory, Mayor Hoffnagel quickly moved to terminate the previous administration's staff and bring in his own people. Hoffnagel's most significant and controversial appointment was that of Angela Donny as the city manager. Donny had an infamous reputation throughout the region.

In twelve years of local city government positions, she had worked in no fewer than eight municipalities. In fact, the International City/County Management Association (ICMA) had investigated her actions a half-dozen times and had issued two public censures. When her past record was revealed to Oakdale citizens, there was an immediate outcry, including many calls for her resignation. Mayor Hoffnagel consequently called an impromptu press conference, at which he made this brief statement:

> I have known Angela for twenty years and worked with her for five. Much like me, she has made and acknowledged her mistakes. Yet, her actions were not criminal, but they were done out of a desire to make changes and improve lives. My administration will not be about waiting, but about evolving. To that end, I ask you to begin the healing process and overlook her early mistakes made out of an over-eagerness to reform.

The mayor had some clear ideas about changing Oakdale and he thought that Donny had the experience and energy to help achieve his vision. A year before Hoffnagel's election, the Oakdale Board of Aldermen discussed a blueprint for the construction of a new city center project. By the time of Hoffnagel's election, the redevelopment project was still in the design phase. At a Board of Aldermen meeting in April 2003, Mayor Hoffnagel, in his typical imperious manner, announced that plans for the redevelopment project needed to be put into action immediately. The Mayor, in his address, appeared anxious and somewhat frustrated that more had not been done with the project. He declared that quicker completion of the complex would save the struggling city. According to the minutes of the meeting, Mayor Hoffman concluded his speech, saying:

> In order to get this project off the ground, I have instructed City Administrator Angela Donny to issue requests for proposals (RFPs) for a project manager. I, under mandatory procedure, will conduct an initial analysis of the project determining its feasibility.

The board was stunned into silence by the mayor's announcement. Surprised by the mayor's unilateral decision, Allen Hauser, a long-time aldermen of Ward II, muttered to nearby Helen Robison, a new alderwoman from Ward III, "We need to watch this guy."

Only a week later, Donny reported that she had not only signed a contract with a project manager, but with an architect as well. The Board of Aldermen along with the Economic Development and Planning and Zoning Committees were taken aback by the almost complete lack of due process and asked to review the RFPs at the April Board of Aldermen meeting in order to determine whether Donny had given all interested parties an equal opportunity to bid on the two contracts. An exhaustive RFP process ensures that the city is not only receiving the best price for the service but that the city is also aware of all its options. Donny responded evasively to the board's request, "I do not have them currently with me, but I will make sure all interested parties will receive them in the near future."

By July, the aldermen, the committees, as well as informed citizens still had not heard from City Administrator Donny regarding the RFP process. When the "old business" section of the agenda was completed, the following dialogue occurred between Alderman Hauser and City Administrator Donny according to the minutes:

HAUSER: Where are the RFPs, Ms. Donny? It has been three months and no one has heard anything. Yet, the plans to begin construction after the acquisition of the land seemed to be moving forward. Where are the RFPs?

DONNY: I do not know. My staff and I have been unable to locate them.

HAUSER: What do you mean? Are they lost?

DONNY: Yes, at the moment. (Hands Hauser form disclosing total cost.)

HAUSER: So, without consulting other administrators, you decided what parties would best complete the job isolating the rest of us from the decision-making process. All you have submitted on this multi-million-dollar project are total costs of more than $300,000.

Donny's inability to produce the missing RFPs proved the last straw for the frustrated aldermen and portended worse to come. The board, now concerned about the redevelopment project that it never approved, asked to see the preliminary analysis supporting the economic feasibility of the project. Mayor Hoffnagel assured the board of the practicality of the endeavor, but the board could not be dissuaded by the mayor's reassuring language. As a result, two independent firms were contracted in July to assess the feasibility of the project, but there was no assurance from either firm that its assessment would be completed before the agreed-upon acquisition of the two properties in September.

As it turned out, the independent firms did not complete their assessments until October. Therefore, the acquisition of the properties for an estimated total of $4.2 million went forward without opposition. When the board and other interested parties received the independent analyses, the aldermen called an emergency meeting in late October to discuss the economic burden the city had assumed. Before anyone had time to address the state of the redevelopment project, Mayor Hoffnagel quickly denounced the independent firms' results as inaccurate and misleading.

The figures from the analyses in front of the board were quite daunting and depressing. The board, after considering these numbers, realized that the city was more than $4 million in debt and moved to terminate the project and sell the recently acquired properties. The mayor quickly responded to the board's action, not directly but through local television, arguing only a few days later that "There are still members in Oakdale's city government who fear change and are scared off by a few obstacles."

After the mayor's statement, the Citizens Review Board (CRB), a voluntary organization composed of appointed residents from local neighborhoods, spoke to the aldermen in a meeting later that month. The CRB argued that the citizens wanted to see the completion of the project because it provided a chance for economic growth and new revenue streams.

As the tension over the issue grew, the ICMA Committee on Professional Conduct instigated another investigation into the practices of City Administrator Donny in February. After only a few weeks, the committee revealed that Donny had failed to ascertain and distribute the proper number of RFPs, employed individuals unqualified for their positions, had not demarcated or updated the responsibilities of her staff, and generally behaved in an unethical manner. Consequently, the committee expelled Donny from her position in the same month. With Donny's termination, it appeared that Mayor Hoffnagel had little room to maneuver.

In March 2004, at a Board of Aldermen meeting, according to the minutes of that night, Aldermen Hauser addressed the situation with Donny and Hoffnagel:

> As I sit here, the city of Oakdale is in bitter turmoil. What began as a project of hope has become one of despair. In what has proven to be unethical violations by former City Administrator Donny and what I believe to be lack of leadership on the part of Mayor Hoffnagel, there is now a schism in the local government and amongst the residents. Mayor Hoffnagel (pointing emphatically in his direction), you once spoke about getting work done, here's your chance!

Later that month, Mayor Hoffnagel resigned from office a broken man, leaving many questions to be answered. For the city of Oakdale, which had been searching for ways to reinvigorate itself, the development project that appeared to be the answer had turned into a major problem.

A CHANGE OF ADMINISTRATION

By June 2004, the Board of Aldermen and the committees had appointed an interim mayor and city administrator until the next elections in 2006. Marie Clarkson, a former city administrator and mayor of a small city in Minnesota, was selected as the interim mayor. Although Clarkson was a credible choice, she had been retired from local city government work for nearly ten years. Since her retirement, Clarkson had become a realtor in the same city she once served. Hauser, a friend of Clarkson's, knew of her success in

Minnesota, and believed that she was the right person to regain the city's balance of authority and direction. Moreover, Paul Asher, who received his graduate and doctoral degrees from local universities, was selected to act as the interim city administrator. Asher, however, had little in the way of practical experience as a city administrator. While in graduate school, he interned under the city administrator. Offered a position after his internship, Asher declined citing a change in careers. He worked on two congressional campaigns and took a position on a politician's staff in Washington, D.C., before returning to the area. He took a job as the city manager of another nearby municipality and had only been there a few months before he received the phone call from Oakdale.

After a week of adjusting to their new roles, Asher and Clarkson corresponded with one another and decided to meet informally to discuss Oakdale's predicament. After pleasantries, Asher quickly got their dialogue focused on Oakdale's redevelopment project.

Since his arrival, Asher had been compiling data in order to redress the economic inefficiencies of the previous administration. Asher relayed to Mayor Clarkson that there were several ways in which this problem could be addressed. Clarkson quickly interrupted Asher to remind him that they were operating against the clock. Not only were the citizens of Oakdale referring to city hall as the "City of Oak-Heads," but developers and interested businesses would be scared off the longer the land sat dormant. Both agreed that a decision had to be made on whether the redevelopment project should proceed or whether it was wiser to shut down the project and find ways to recoup expenditures. Mayor Clarkson explained to Asher that she would call an emergency meeting in the first week of August at which the fate of the project would be decided. This gave Asher one month to find a solution to the multi tiered problem. After they shook hands, Asher walked to his car feeling that the weight of this decision was on his shoulders.

As soon as Asher returned from his meeting, he sat down at his desk, took a sip of cold coffee, and began to chart out the implications of either choice. If he ruled in favor of the decision to proceed with the redevelopment project, then there were both positive and negative outcomes. On the positive side, the redevelopment would increase morale and confidence within the community. It would help keep and attract local businesses. If it was not funded, it would hurt future project proposals. On the negative, as a result of the financial burden of the project, the quality of municipal services would be lower or taxes would need to be raised. For example, in order for the redevelopment project to be completed successfully, all unassigned general funds would have to be directed toward the services related to the complex. According to independent auditors, the Public Works and Police Departments were an estimated $30,000 over budget in 2004. Cuts would have to be made, but where?

Asher leaned back in his chair, rubbed his face with both hands, and as his weary eyes readjusted, they caught a glance of something that he kept framed on the wall of his office. As he gazed at the picture frame, Asher recalled the part of the conversation with Clarkson when they discussed the previous administration's ethical lapses. He realized that just as important to the city's reputation as good fiscal management was restoring the city government's integrity. He walked to the left of his desk and looked at the City Administrator's Code of Ethics, the object that was framed on his wall.

Asher was reminded by the code that his decision would ultimately affect the well-being of the residents of Oakdale for not just this year or next but for many years to come. What would be the best way to present the facts of the case to the residents and give them an opportunity to offer their input? Furthermore, it is his duty to make the most fiscally responsible choices for the city. Gambling on a project that may or may not succeed is a bet using the tax money of Oakdale citizens. The analysis was creating a great deal of stress so he went to the window in his office, leaned against it, and began working out the details. Ultimately, if they did proceed with the project, the procedural steps would have to be completed fully and accurately, allowing residents to regain confidence in their government while creating an opportunity for generating new revenues.

On the other hand, if the project was terminated, Asher would be unpopular with the citizens, at least, initially. Then again, the property could be sold, minimizing the city's losses, and a new project, that was better conceived and more transparent in its planning, could be started. At that very moment, a ringing tone came from his computer, which was a signal that he had just received an e-mail. Out of habit, Asher walked over to check it. It read:

TO: City Administrator Paul Asher

FROM: Aldermen Allen Hauser

RE: NW/SW Redevelopment Project

I just spoke with Mayor Clarkson about ten minutes ago. She told me the content of your conversation. I agree that something needs to be done to clear up the mess created by Hoffnagel and Donny. But, I will be honest with you: the Board of Aldermen is really torn on this issue. We will be really looking toward you for guidance.

Sincerely,

Allen Hauser

The burden of this problem thus continued to grow. With the content of the e-mail in the back of his mind, Asher began to hash out another scenario. He thought that if he rejected the project outright, then it might hamper other growth opportunities in the future. Asher was tired, and at this point, he turned off his computer, went to his office door, and turned off the light to head home.

When the day of the August meeting arrived, Asher got up, put on his suit, toasted a bagel, and headed to Oakdale City Hall. As he pulled into his parking space, he noticed that there was a large turnout of citizens. Once he arrived within the building and everyone settled, the meeting commenced. After the formalities, the resolution for the redevelopment project came up for discussion.

Alderman Hauser read the proposal on whether the redevelopment project should proceed or be terminated. Hauser turned first to Paul Asher and asked, "City Administrator Paul Asher, what do you have to say on this issue?"

Discussion Questions

1. How would you address the building problem if you were in Asher's position? Explain.

2. As city administrator, how should professional and personal ethics inform your actions in this case?

3. Being a nonelected official, how can Asher be effective as a city administrator in the local political environment (including the press and interest groups)?

4. Was the use of authority in procuring contracts for a project manager and an architect an individual, departmental, or systemic problem? Why?

5. How should Asher address Oakdale's fiscal issues? What would be his most effective course of action? Why?

APPENDIX A

City of Oakdale Organizational Chart

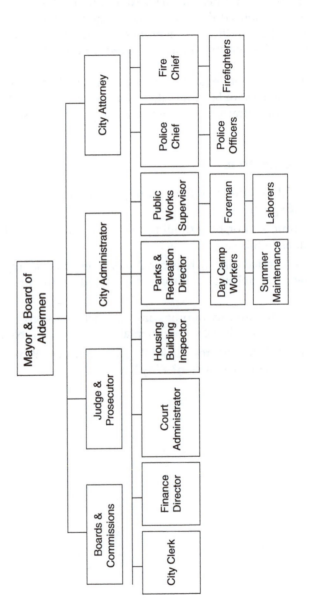

12 | GRASSROOTS CHANGE INITIATIVES CASE

Jennifer M. Giancola,
Robert A. Cropf, and
Illana Barash

OVERVIEW

Abstract

This case examines differences in the purpose and business approach of the private, public, and nonprofit sectors. These differing viewpoints and practices clash as one employee attempts to bring about change at a nonprofit organization. Sue Thompson is the new assistant director at a nonprofit grassroots organization with the purpose of protecting the public interest through collective student and community action. Sue's commitment quickly wanes as she uncovers a number of problems, including high turnover, inefficient and ineffective practices, and poor financial management. Sue suggests conducting an evaluation and tries to make small improvements, but ultimately she experiences strong philosophical differences with the executive director and office manager.

Main Topics

Decision making, Implementation/evaluation

Secondary Topics

Democracy, Privatization

Teaching Purpose

To discuss nonprofit administration and debate business practices in private, public, and nonprofit organizations in the context of a grassroots advocacy organization

The Organization

The case examines a nonprofit, grassroots organization whose mission is to protect the public interest.

Main Characters

- Sue Thompson, Assistant Director
- Jackson Tyler, Executive Director
- Emily Lambeth, Office Manager

BACKGROUND

The Grassroots Change Initiative (GCI) is an advocacy group that is a local chapter of the umbrella group the United States Grassroots Change Initiatives (USGCI). USGCI was created in the 1980s to act as a watchdog for the public interest in our nation's capital, just as the state offices have worked to safeguard the public interest in state capitals since the early 1970s. USGCI's mission is to advocate for consumers' rights, the natural environment, and other progressive causes. This mission includes delivering persistent, results-oriented, public-interest activism that protects our environment; encourages a fair, sustainable economy; and fosters a responsive democratic government. Some of USGCI's most recent campaigns have included stopping Congress from opening the Arctic National Wildlife Refuge to drilling and playing a pivotal role in convincing congressional representatives to vote down an environmentally harmful energy bill despite the powerful utility and energy industries backing the proposal.

MISSION AND STRUCTURE OF GCI

GCI is a student-run organization that is affiliated with local colleges and universities. Specifically, its mission statement is

> The Grassroots Change Initiative (GCI) is created to empower students to take charge in local communities to work on behalf of citizens' interest.

GCI has two offices within the state; however, this case study will focus on the original office site, which has been in existence for more than twenty-five years. This office is located in the heart of an eclectic area known for a young, trendy, educated crowd that likes to spend its weekends in coffee shops during the day and sushi or wine bars during the night. GCI chose this location in order to appeal to the local clientele, a group of people who believe that nonprofits can make a difference in our world and who are well educated with high disposable incomes.

The office is located next to a flower shop and a vodka/sushi bar. Upon entering, there is a tall staircase lined with old political posters and fact sheets about various current events, mostly about global warming and corporate giants. There are two rooms in the office: an "office" and a main room. The office is essentially made up of file cabinets overflowing with past campaign materials, stickers, binders, fact sheets, an old fax machine, an old black-and-white copier, and a desk. Clearly, this is not a room to be seen by the public. The main room is also lined with various political posters and fact sheets. There is a large paper thermometer on one wall, on which the staff members mark their monetary goals each day, adorned with the names of the people who made the most money the previous afternoon. There are also tons of campaign materials strewn about the room, stuck in book shelves, and spewing out of file cabinets or boxes. Random instructions and directions are posted above the three desks sitting in the corner of the main room, reserved for campaign managers and directors.

The office experiences a great deal of turnover at the management level. It has new campaign managers every few weeks, a new office director approximately every year, and a new campaign approximately every four months. Some of its most recent campaigns have included the "Campaign to Save the Environment," in which it sought to inform people and raise money for global warming research, student aid, consumer debt, and harmful toys campaigns. Although USGCI and state GCIs support various political issues, there is no specific endorsement of political candidates.

GCI employs individuals who go door-to-door and talk to citizens about important current events and ask them to get involved financially. Literally, each employee spends about five hours each afternoon walking up and down streets in various neighborhoods, knocking on every door, presenting a three-minute speech about the issue of the day, and asking for money. This is done during the hours of 4 p.m. to 9 p.m., but a vast portion of the target population is not home when the canvasser arrives. Hence, GCI requires each canvasser to double back through his or her assigned neighborhood and re-approach every door at which there was no answer. Frankly, these canvassers behave the same as solicitors who call during dinner time. GCI, however, makes it very clear that they are not solicitors because they are not selling anything. If there is a "no soliciting" sign on someone's door, then canvassers are recommended to try away.

Most of the employees are students looking for a socially rewarding part-time job, but there are occasionally employees who come to GCI with the false impression that the organization can offer them a stable income and employment. This is one of the primary problems with GCI: it advertises itself as a group that can help save the environment and offers its workers a set sum of money each week, but what it does not advertise is its paychecks are commission based and overtime is required.

Some GCI employees are responsible for organizing press conferences or heading up letter writing campaigns for publication in local newspapers. Unfortunately, there is a massive breakdown of communication permeating the organization, from both the top down and across the span of control of campaign managers or canvass directors. As a result of this lack of organization and refusal to implement any standard operating procedures, the local GCI falls incredibly short of its potential and rarely meets campaign goals.

NEW ASSISTANT DIRECTOR

Sue had been working in finance in the private sector for the past four years since graduating from college. Although she enjoyed her job, she was looking for a change and for a place where she could "make a difference." When she saw the job ad for an assistant director of GCI, she was excited and thought that she had found the answer.

When Sue showed up for her initial interview at GCI, she assumed the experience would parallel her previous job interviews, so she was dressed in business-casual attire and arrived with a few copies of her résumé in hand. Upon walking into the office, Sue realized this interview was nothing like what

she was expecting. There were four metal folding chairs arranged in a semicir-
cle around a television, and she was clearly overdressed for the occasion. Emily,
the office manager, explained to Sue that they were running behind schedule so
Sue was welcome to take a seat and wait, or she could come back in an hour.
Not quite sure of the proper protocol in this organization, Sue assumed it would
be best not to leave. As she waited for her interview to begin, Sue tried not to
eavesdrop while Emily answered phones and argued about the GCI budget.

The interview began with a short fifteen-minute introduction video,
explaining what it means to work for Grassroots Change Initiative. Then,
Emily had Sue and three other applicants fill out some basic paperwork and
then called each person into the "office" separately. Emily looked at Sue's
résumé and paperwork and immediately offered Sue the position as assistant
director. They discussed pay and hours, and Sue eagerly accepted the job.
What Emily failed to mention was that pay is essentially commission based,
and the hours of 2 p.m. to 10 p.m. are a minimum requirement, because most
managers had to be at the office around 11 a.m. each day for preparations and
other administrative tasks. It was also assumed that everyone would go out for
a social activity afterward, at least until midnight. On Wednesday nights, GCI
sponsored "pizza nights" and the money came out of the campaign funds.

Sue began work the following week. Emily set her up at her desk with
little direction. In fact, it was a couple of days before Sue met with her boss,
Jackson, the executive director. The two of them really hit it off at their first
meeting. Jackson was very laid back and wore casual clothes and sandals to
the office. He made Sue feel right at home and got her excited about the
mission of GCI—a mission about which Jackson clearly felt passionate.

PROBLEMS AT GCI

After six months in her position, Sue realized that there were many problems
with GCI that had to be solved before any sort of productive and positive
political action could be taken and before any public policies could be impacted.
There was a complete breakdown in the efficiency and effectiveness among GCI
students and staff in accomplishing goals. This was a common occurrence in
most state GCI offices because, in part, few people stayed with the organization
very long. The bulk of "employees" were volunteers or low-paid student
workers. The turnover rate was so high that staff of GCI became more con-
sumed with attracting and maintaining employees than with its mission work.
As the focus of the entire organization turned to how much money could be
raised through door-to-door canvassing, other means of advocacy fell by the
wayside. Responsibilities such as holding press conferences and writing letters
to the editor were essentially ignored because there was not enough time.

Also, the means of fund-raising were incredibly archaic and ineffective.
Canvassers were asked to spend five hours each day walking door-to-door and
asking citizens to provide monthly financial donations for various causes, rang-
ing from the Campaign to Save the Environment to the Human Rights Campaign.
Prior to heading out to neighborhoods, canvassers had to spend at least two

hours practicing role-plays and attempting to attract future employees and another hour having lunch as a "team." These three hours were not paid, but employees were still held to many of the GCI rules during them, including no smoking while wearing GCI attire, staying with the group, and focusing on how to talk to people at their door. Despite the obvious inefficiencies of going door-to-door at 4 p.m. when no one is home or during the dinner hour, such practices were not changed because "that was the way things had always been done."

Sue was concerned that GCI was not fulfilling its mission and the original intent of USGCIs and to make matters worse, an evaluation had never been conducted at GCI. Nonetheless, she attempted to make incremental changes throughout the GCI office but faced one obstacle after another. Many of Sue's modifications included simply trying to properly train canvassers. She worked with them to improve communication and "sales" skills with potential givers. She tried to run the daily schedule in a more effective manner so that time was not wasted. Sue believed that simple organizational improvements and clearer communication would save much time and confusion. Unfortunately, the idealism Sue initially had upon beginning her employment at GCI quickly wore off as she observed the necessity for, and continued avoidance of, more business-like management within GCI's office.

Jackson recognized Sue's frustration and attempted to improve her morale by setting up standing meetings with her. The objective was to work together to write letters to the editor, build media packets about local issues, and so on. Sue would arrive at the office early, eager to actually put her college degree to use, but Jackson rarely followed through. He would be late or distracted or would cancel meetings. Rather than getting angrier, Sue decided to write letters herself. But Jackson never read them, and eventually Sue stopped writing them.

In an attempt to keep Sue around longer, Emily gave Sue more responsibilities, including reviewing some of GCI's budget. After hours of examining the spreadsheets, Sue saw that GCI was operating with only $60 over expenses. Furthermore, less than 40 percent of all funds raised actually went toward lobbying efforts, programs, and political information, a very low number for an advocacy group. Sue was infuriated that all of the canvassers' hard work was resulting in so little going to the "cause." She had signed on for this cause in order to make a difference, not help pay the rent of a run-down building and help recruit more part-time workers. She no longer felt invested in the mission statement of GCI because she was struggling to see it put into action.

PHILOSOPHICAL DIFFERENCES

The budget problem was the final straw for Sue. She decided to call a meeting with Emily and Jackson to air her frustrations in hopes of agreeing on a plan of action to improve GCI. At the meeting, Sue explained that she did not feel as if GCI had made a solid impact around the area. She spent more of her time training people, many of whom rarely stayed through the week, and answering phones than writing press releases or organizing campaigns. Furthermore,

GCI was barely making enough money to survive, let alone achieve its goals and make a difference.

Emily and Jackson, however, did not agree with Sue's perspective. Jackson firmly believed that GCI was serving a lofty purpose that went beyond just making money. "Isn't that why we are a nonprofit?" he gently asked. He went on to say that GCI exists to protect the public interest and that there are many citizens who want to volunteer and be a part of organizations such as theirs. Although Emily agreed with Jackson's views regarding a mission-driven organization that was integral to civil society, she had a different philosophy on how it should operate. Not only did she think that it did not need to run like a business, but also she thought that the government should supplement GCI's operating revenue. She stated, "After all, we are working for public interest and supporting students to be publicly minded citizens."

Sue believed, on the other hand, that the GCI idea of a nonprofessional management style was not conducive to an efficiently and effectively run organization. As more and more people began to realize this, they walked away from this organization in hopes of seeking more effective and efficient means of attaining political change. Sue's intent was not to discredit the use of grassroots campaigning, but to highlight the need for effective management of such campaigns. Sue argued, "Idealism and wanting to make a difference are great in nonprofit organizations, but they must be balanced with some proper business and management administration." Sue suggested that the first step was to design and implement a program evaluation that included process and impact assessments. From there, a plan for change could be developed.

Emily and Jackson become defensive at the suggestion of an evaluation. A heated debate ensued.

Discussion Questions

1. How would you characterize the philosophical differences among Sue, Jackson, and Emily? What do you see as the strengths and weaknesses of their varying viewpoints?

2. How can Sue bring about positive change at GCI? What suggestions would you make to enhance GCI?

3. What steps should be taken in the design and implementation of a program evaluation at GCI? What research methods and assessments would you suggest for assessing efficiency and effectiveness?

4. How do the values and missions of nonprofit organizations differ from other organizations and/or agencies in the private and public sectors?

5. How can a balance be achieved between running an organization through the lens of business administration compared to running it through the lens of public administration?

6. Can a more business-like approach contribute to the GCI's grassroots' effectiveness? Explain.

13 COMMUNITY HEALTH CENTER CASE

Jennifer M. Giancola,
Robert A. Cropf, and
Jacquelynn Orr

OVERVIEW

Abstract

This case demonstrates the importance of aligning strategic and operational plans with environmental needs. It examines For the People (FTP), a community health center that is part of a larger health provider, DUNN Community Care. FTP faces a rapidly changing environment and needs to adapt quickly to remain viable. However, the parent organization, DUNN, is obstructing some much-needed changes such as participation in the Governor's Change Initiative. The FTP director, Miranda Jackson, knows her organization needs to innovate to survive but lacks the financial and human resources and political support to enact new strategies.

Main Topics

Planning, Strategic management

Secondary Topics

Reform, Organizational culture

Teaching Purpose

To encourage students to think at a macro level by discussing the development, implementation, and communication of a strategic plan in an organization

The Organization

The case examines a community health center that is part of a larger nonprofit health care organization.

Main Characters

- Miranda Jackson, Director of FTP
- DUNN Board of Directors

BACKGROUND

Community health centers were developed to address complex issues related to disparities in access and care within the American health care system. There are now more than 1,000 federally funded community health centers throughout various underserved communities in the United States. Over the past forty years, community health centers have expanded; today's community health center network is one of the nation's largest primary care systems.

For the People (FTP) is the largest community health center operating under the multifaceted, nonprofit health care provider DUNN Community Care. The FTP facility is on a main thoroughfare with good access to public transportation and other services, and it is the only Federally Qualified Health Center (FQHC) in its service area. FQHCs are community owned and operated health centers for the underprivileged. Because it is an FQHC, FTP can work directly with Medicare and Medicaid, as well as apply for federal funding to support the organization.

For more than 40 years, FTP has been serving a large urban community of nearly 2.5 million residents. FTP's target population is the more than 575,000 uninsured and underinsured residents from various backgrounds and minority groups, 95 percent of whom live at or below 200 percent of the federal poverty level. When the health center was first opened, patient care was provided in a modest double-wide trailer; now FTP and DUNN have more than ten large medical clinics, twenty school-based centers, and a number of other medical facilities in their network.

DUNN STRATEGY

FTP has a director who is responsible for overseeing the health center, but who must ultimately answer to the DUNN Board of Directors. Since DUNN is designated as a FQHC, the organization is required to be governed by a community board with a patient majority—that is, a majority that reflects the population the health center serves.

Three years ago, the Board decided that the entire organization needed to examine its strategy and goals. On a national level, health care costs were going up, and the number of people without adequate insurance was becoming a salient political issue. At an organizational level, the Board realized that all the DUNN affiliates were going to have to begin operating more efficiently if they were to survive.

The Board hired an outside consulting firm to assist with the facilitation of an extensive strategic planning process. The planning committee included the board members who met for a two-day retreat to devise a plan for the entire organization. The process included collecting and reviewing data from various stakeholder groups. A SWOT analysis was conducted to help determine the strategic direction and goals of the organization. In the SWOT, the board looked at internal strengths and weaknesses and external opportunities and threats to determine leverage points and strategic direction. The DUNN

Board and outside consultants established three strategic priorities focused on patients and employees:

a. Eliminating health disparities and improving access;
b. Delivering quality-driven and cost-effective primary and preventative care; and
c. Facilitating economic and community development of the service area.

In addition to these strategic priorities, the Board decided to pursue a stability strategy. This would ensure that the organization remains the same size and meets stakeholders' needs while cutting costs. Given that not all parts of the DUNN organization have the same structure and needs, the Board allowed for some flexibility on the individual health center level. The centers were given the strategic plan and directed to develop "business-level" goals and tactical plans.

FTP'S BUSINESS STRATEGY

Whereas the DUNN board is concerned with the long-term viability of the parent organization, the FTP director and staff are busy trying to make sure that their particular clinic excels. FTP can concentrate on this goal because the DUNN Board has given each business unit the authority to "address the competitive aspect" of each facility by allowing the directors to develop their own business strategies. Hence, FTP creates its own sub-strategy to tailor planning efforts to its unique situation. Although it functions independently, FTP must work within the vision and mission of the larger organization.

FTP has used its freedom to define itself as a different sort of health care center: one that offers superb care and respectful treatment to all patients, no matter their background. The organization has presented itself as a quality-care provider for the uninsured or the underinsured, who together comprise up to 64 percent of FTP patients. To date, the differentiation strategy has been successful for FTP and has translated into satisfied patients who consistently return to the facility. In a recent patient satisfaction survey, more than 90 percent of surveyed patients reported high approval of FTP facilities and its staff.

Although FTP has adopted a differentiation strategy on the business level, the individual service departments have used a low-cost strategy that incorporates corporate- (DUNN) and business- (FTP) level strategies. The administrative team also adopted a "low cost ≠ low quality" mantra, encouraging FTP staff to deliver top-notch care at the lowest cost possible.

A NEED FOR INNOVATION

Just a few years after the Board engaged in the strategic planning overhaul, Miranda Jackson, FTP's director, began to feel that DUNN's priorities matched less and less with the challenges FTP was confronting. Since the strategic plan was implemented, Jackson and many of her health center employees began to observe a drastic shift in the makeup of their community and clients. A majority of the people coming into the clinic were non-English-speaking (mostly Haitian-Creole and Spanish), most were not U.S. citizens, and many did not possess appropriate immigration documents.

Despite some obstacles, FTP had a number of strengths. A $500,000 exterior renovation project was completed six months earlier. FTP's status as one of the community's best employers helped in the recruitment and retention of staff. Over the past two years, the local Department of Health had provided a $20,000 subsidy for operational costs. And, new funding streams from automated Medicaid managed care plans and new health care legislation were on the horizon.

Although Miranda and the FTP administrative team wanted to adopt DUNN's "low-cost" policy during this time, employees were complaining that some costs were simply unmanageable because of the changing clientele. There was a need for trained staff members to act as translators for the medical and administrative staff, and often the clinic had to seek legal council to deal with immigration issues that could impair access to or quality of care. Most FTP employees truly wanted to help their clients, but they felt a great deal of pressure to achieve the financial and competitive goals promoted by DUNN's leadership.

The corporate office for DUNN did not address the need for innovation or aggressiveness that Miranda knew was indispensible in the competitive and dynamic health care field. The Board's inability to address these elements was compromising FTP's ability to remain competitive and viable within its service areas. As a result, Miranda began to actively go to DUNN's Board to inform it of what was needed to serve FTP's target population. Unfortunately, the Board was slow to respond to Miranda's requests. She became frustrated that the Board could not produce more innovative strategies to deal with FTP's rapidly changing environment.

GOVERNOR'S CHANGE INITIATIVE

Miranda and the team of grant writers at FTP were always looking for new government programs that could improve their organization. When one of the staff members presented Miranda with a new state program supporting innovative programs, she was eager to learn more. The Governor's Change Initiative, specifically, was designed to help organizations meet the needs of the changing health care environment. This seemed like a perfect way for Miranda to fund the strategic changes that needed to occur at FTP without financially burdening DUNN.

Miranda submitted a Governor's Change Initiative proposal to the DUNN Board for approval with the goal of being the alpha test site for new strategies within the organization. Miranda hoped that implementing these strategies would make FTP more competitive and adaptable. She and the staff were excited that making some simple changes could ultimately provide better patient care. Much to their dismay, however, the DUNN Board of Directors did not immediately approve the proposal.

Miranda knew that the strategic and tactical recommendations in the Governor's Change Initiative were important for FTP's survival. Forecasted results confirmed that FTP was at risk of losing a large amount of their market share in the next five years, because of both a lack of community partnerships and a loss of government funding opportunities. Neither FTP nor DUNN had any financial or operational partnerships with any of the local hospitals or community health centers, and another prominent community health care organization had lost government funding three years earlier and had been forced to close. Although the DUNN Board tried to engage in strategic planning for the benefit of the organization, it had consistently failed to take these kinds of environmental factors into account during the planning sessions. Miranda believed that implementing the Governor's Change Initiative was a risk worth taking, and that the Board was hindering FTP's ability to innovate and adapt.

After another disappointing conference call with DUNN board members, Miranda returned to her office, worried about the future of the organization she cared for so much. She expected the Governor's Change Initiative, with its financial modifications and new management techniques, to provide FTP's administration and staff with the opportunity to evaluate and implement various creative options for delivering quality services while implementing a new strategic and financial plan. However, the reliance of DUNN leadership on the traditions of the organization instead of addressing emerging trends could contribute to a significant loss of market share and potential funding opportunities in the near future for the entire organization. DUNN's efforts at strategic planning did not seem to reflect the issues that were so obvious to the FTP director and staff. With new funding streams would probably come more competition for those funds, and Miranda was ambivalent about whether or not the DUNN Board could weather the increasingly turbulent health care environment. Miranda was in a bind: she could almost touch what needed to be done, but because of the Board's inertia, it was just beyond her grasp.

Discussion Questions

1. Why do you think the Board opposes Miranda's recommendations? Do you think it is a reasonable position for the Board to take? Explain.

2. Does FTP have a real need to change its strategy? Explain.

3. What action steps would you suggest for Miranda to meet conflicting stakeholder needs, including those of the Board and FTP clientele?

4. What suggestions would you give to DUNN to improve future strategic planning processes? How could it better communicate and implement the plan throughout the entire organization?

5. How can DUNN better align its strategy with the health care environment? How can it better align the strategy with the internal structure and culture?

14 | COMMUNITY CREDIT UNION

Robert A. Cropf,
Jennifer M. Giancola, and
Paul Woodruff

OVERVIEW

Abstract

A nonprofit or public organization faces a wide range of issues and responsibilities regarding its dealings with consumers of its services. In the following case, the lending policies of a credit union toward the low-income households it serves come under close scrutiny. This case study asks whether it is the responsibility of a public organization to help its customers take more control over their own lives, in this instance, their financial situation.

Main Topics

Social equity, Implementation/evaluation

Secondary Topics

Financial management

Teaching Purpose

To examine the dilemma organizations face in dealing with low-income clients when the choice is between meeting immediate needs versus long-term education for financial responsibility

The Organization

Community Credit Union (CCU) is a nonprofit organization with a commitment to higher customer service, including offering loans at lower interest rates than for-profit banking institutions.

Main Characters

- Cortez McDuffy, Lead Teller at a CCU Branch Bank
- Alma Murphy, Customer
- Lucinda Tassels, Branch Manager
- Molly Salamone, CCU President
- Paul Woodbine, Former Credit Union Bank President

BACKGROUND

Credit unions are nonprofit financial institutions, typically composed of persons who share a characteristic, such as living in a certain geographic region; membership in professional associations or private corporations; or employment as civil servants within local, state, or federal government. The capital of credit unions comes from the purchase of shares by members, who in turn receive dividends based on their investment. Unlike other banks, credit unions are not driven by profit motives. Instead, they are committed to providing a higher quality of customer service and issuing loans at lower interest rates to their members than do for-profit banks.

Within the Centreville metropolitan area, the Community Credit Union (CCU) is a rapidly expanding financial institution, with a mission to provide a high level of services to its members. In Community's case, each member pays a nominal $5 fee to join. Everyone who banks with Community is treated as a stakeholder and beneficiary of its future success or failure. According to its mission, success is based on two criteria: customer satisfaction and the credit union's ability to provide appropriate products and advice for members to grow their wealth and to achieve a certain level of financial responsibility. These commitments are summed up by a phrase the institution's management uses: "To serve the community without profit or charity."

CCU traces its origin to members of the Centreville Suburban Teachers Association (CSTA). As time went on, membership and total assets of the cooperative grew rapidly, spurring the credit union to change its name to Educational Employees Credit Union (EECU). The new name reflected expanding membership eligibility to those outside the teaching profession and away from the immediate metropolitan region. EECU continued to merge with smaller educational credit unions until it combined with Universal Credit Union (whose membership included manufacturing employees). Finally, the institution's name was changed to Community Credit Union to more accurately describe the diverse membership of the organization.

In order to maintain a competitive edge with rival credit unions and for-profit banks, CCU strives to offer a wide variety of special services to its membership. However, one service in particular, Courtesy Pay (C-Pay), has come under sharp criticism by some inside and outside the organization. C-Pay is designed to prevent extra fees and the embarrassment that can result for members who overdraw their accounts either by bouncing a check or using their debit card. If a check or debit exceeds what is in their account, Community will cover the transaction up to $300. However, with this coverage comes a $25 fee. This is a lower price compared to the extra costs members would incur from other financial institutions; other banks would also assess a fee for the returned check or debited item.

The problem with this program is that some members have discovered how to use C-Pay in a way that was not intended by the credit union. For example, members who have a zero balance in their checking account are still qualified to receive the benefits of the C-Pay system. All they need to do is go to a branch and write a check to themselves for $275. The $25 fee is taken from the Courtesy Pay reserve, and the remaining $275 is given to the member. Before they can access this again, however, they must repay any outstanding loans. Nonetheless, members can repeat this process over and over again, without facing penalties, as long as they repay the debt.

THE CASE OF ALMA MURPHY

Lead teller Cortez McDuffy describes her experiences with one member, Alma Murphy, who is representative of others who abuse the C-Pay privilege. "Alma always has a very low account balance, if any at all. Also, any loans she has are usually late in being paid. She is a nice lady so I let her come in and do this. She uses the program a couple times a month on average."

CCU President Molly Salamone echoed these sentiments and added, "The financial situation for members like Alma isn't good. They don't seem to have their priorities straight when it comes to their finances."

Alma is employed in a low-income job as an assistant office manager in a small factory. She is trying to raise two grandchildren, largely on her own—she does receive some government support. Her daughter is in prison on a drug charge, and the father left the family long before. As might be expected, her life is hard, but Alma is not one to complain. She refuses anything that might be construed as a handout and is determined in her effort to raise her grandchildren by herself and not allow them to go into foster care.

McDuffy went on to say, "Members like Alma think C-Pay is a line of credit even though it definitely isn't. There is one member with us who had fifty-one returned items (checks or debits) from last year. Currently, she is at forty-three returned items for the year. She could not have accidentally overdrawn her account that many times. Alma isn't as bad but she does return items more than the average member. Also, people don't pay attention to the fees because they're living week to week."

"Some of our members think C-Pay is a service to be accessed anytime they want and that it's there to be abused. If people were properly educated about the financial consequences of their actions, maybe they would use it less," stated Salamone.

When asked if she has done anything to dissuade members like Alma from using the service, Salamone said that she often tells them about the credit union's overdraft line of credit (LOC) service, which charges an annual interest rate that is much less than the automatic $25 fee for each bounced item. However, many of the people like Alma who intentionally access C-Pay often do not qualify for lines of credit because of low credit scores. Concerning LOC referrals, McDuffy said that even if members did qualify for this overdraft service, "they would just max it out and still access their C-Pay." He continued, "Since this is a service designed to help members who inadvertently overdraw their account, members with excessive use of this service should be counseled on managing their checking account in a more responsive manner."

But no mention is made of what constitutes "excessive use," who will guide members to counseling, or who will provide this counseling.

In addition to the rules for the C-Pay system, CCU is guided by its mission statement, organizational values, and a member pledge. Particularly, the pledge contains four points that seem to contradict the organization's decision to allow members to use C-Pay as a line of credit. These include the promise to understand customers' financial needs to help them with their financial understanding and to promote financial solutions and security.

If an important part of CCU's mission is to truly help its members to become more financially responsible, then it should be asking Alma and other people who overuse C-Pay to seek financial counseling. However, taking this course of action poses some significant challenges to the organization. Branch Manager Lucinda Tassels, for example, said that Community does not possess the infrastructure and tools needed to help members better understand the long-term financial repercussions of using C-pay frequently.

Additionally, the contact that managers and financial service representatives (FSRs) have with members is more limited than the frequent interactions that they have with tellers in their day-to-day banking business. When tellers notice a problem, they often refer members to LOCs. However, as stated previously, many members do not have high enough credit scores to qualify for this service. In other instances, tellers counsel members to discuss their situation with FSRs or managers and to talk about the fees that they incur with C-Pay as well as ways to prevent them. This places the decision to seek help entirely in the hands of the members. If they choose not to seek help, there is currently little the credit union can do.

Even though tellers are on the "front lines" in dealing with customers, they are not asked to provide input in any meaningful way to the decision making of upper-level management. It is not that the managers refuse to listen to the tellers, the tellers just do not routinely give advice to their bosses regarding what they view as administrative matters nor do the managers ask the tellers for their suggestions.

COMMUNITY CREDIT UNION MISSION AND VALUES

CCU is a nonprofit organization that takes very seriously its commitment to members and the larger community. Tellers, supervisors, and branch managers at CCU are supposed to help members manage their finances in a responsible way. For the most part, this does happen and is a reason why CCU has grown to its large size today. As its motto, "To serve the community without profit or charity," suggests, this is an organization that tries to put its patrons first.

Tassels said that CCU is a place where "people help people." She added, "Putting people further in debt through C-Pay isn't helping them. But, on a service level, we can fulfill their needs by helping them pay their bills."

Salamone agreed with these sentiments by adding, "Our credit union is designed to help people. C-Pay, like it or not, does this by allowing them to pay their bills. But, it also seems like we're helping them to get one step ahead only to bring them a few steps behind when they are continually paying these fees."

Thus, it appears that employees at CCU have mixed feelings about the use of C-Pay, which pits the credit union mission against serving the short-term needs of its members. Although CCU views itself as a proactive organization in terms of serving the community, in this instance, it seems to promote a policy that encourages its members to behave in ways that are antithetical to its service pledges.

Despite the caring organizational culture that CCU tries to foster, there are some questions behind its deeper motives involving C-Pay. Nonprofits, despite their name, still have to make money to survive and continue to offer their services to the public.

Paul Woodbine, a former credit union bank president says, "In contrast with for-profit banking centers, credit unions impose very few fees on their patrons. Aside from monetary penalties for failure to make loan payments in a timely manner and non-sufficient funds (NSF) fees for returned or overdrawn items, few charges are assessed. As a result, the few fee sources are all the more important."

Thus C-Pay, whether intentionally or unintentionally, is one of the largest moneymakers for CCU. If four people intentionally access their C-Pay at any branch in one day, the salary for one part-time teller for one day has been covered. In a week's time, at least fifteen to twenty, if not more, of these transactions will take place at each one of the branch locations. In the case of the member who had fifty-one NSF fees in a year, the credit union received $1,275. That's the equivalent of 127.5 hours paid for a part-time teller making $10 an hour. Thus CCU, although nominally committed to member service, can little afford to implement a policy of aggressively preventing members from overdrawing their accounts; if it did so, the organization would stand to lose hundreds of thousands, if not millions, of dollars in income from this single fee.

Woodbine said, "This is the trap for credit unions. They either charge the fees and look the other way or they have to raise their prices for their basic services."

Tassels admitted that C-Pay is a moneymaker for CCU, but she also stands by her belief that the credit union is helping a vulnerable segment of the population. "Without C-Pay, these people would have nothing, maybe payday loans, but that's worse than nothing in my book."

President Salamone agreed, saying, "Granted, C-Pay is often abused and a strong case can be made for financial counseling. However, let's look at the reality of these people's daily lives. These are often hard-working family people without a lot of resources. They need the money for rent and groceries. They're not going out and spending their C-Pay on drugs or booze. Until something better comes along, this is the best alternative to the price-gouging payday lenders. Yes, they do need counseling but ask yourself if you were in their shoes, which is the rational decision, food for the grandkids or financial responsibility?"

EVALUATION OF C-PAY

Woodbine, the former bank president, suggested one solution that would entail an evaluation of the credit union's C-Pay policy. In this way, CCU could rationally weigh the pros and cons of retaining C-Pay. A simple benefit-cost analysis would look at measuring the benefits and costs of C-Pay in dollars. The decision rule would then be straightforward and easy to apply: if C-Pay's benefits exceed its costs in terms of dollars, then the program should be retained. However, the following question arises: Whose benefits and costs should be included? Thus, as seen earlier, C-Pay has clear monetary benefits for CCU and also for the members. But how does one include the long-term costs of financial irresponsibility on the part of customers? Another issue that would need to be addressed is how are intangible benefits and costs to be included? For instance, how does one measure the benefits of members learning how to become more responsible in their financial planning? What are the social costs or benefits of C-Pay? In other words, does C-Pay's encourage fee paying instead of saving?

Discussion Questions

1. Do you believe Tassels and Salamone when they imply that CCU is living up to its member pledge and core principles in allowing members to intentionally access the C-Pay system? What are the implications of your answer for organizational transparency?

2. Should the tellers have more of a role in CCU's decision making? Explain.

3. How would you evaluate CCU's C-Pay? What would be your criteria for successful outcomes?

4. Suppose you are on the board of directors for CCU. You have just heard a presentation regarding the C-Pay program. The board has been asked to consider a fundamental change to the system that would prevent members from intentionally bouncing checks to access their C-Pay. Would you support this proposal? Why or why not?

5. What are some of the potential drawbacks or advantages for CCU if this change were adopted and implemented? Explain.

APPENDIX A

COMMUNITY CREDIT UNION

Simplified Organizational Chart

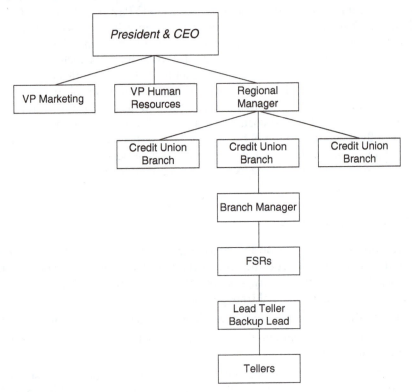

APPENDIX B

C-Pay Regulations and Criteria

Courtesy Pay is a service designed to help the members avoid additional fees if they inadvertently overdraw their account.

Courtesy Pay *is not* a Line of Credit. It is literally a courtesy that we will extend to our members (whose accounts meet certain requirements) to save them the embarrassment and inconvenience of returned item(s) as well as costly fees that merchants normally charge for items returned to them.

Here is how Courtesy Pay works:

After members exhaust their Overdraft Protection Line of Credit and/or Regular Savings, (subject to REG D), we may, at our discretion, honor the member's overdraft transaction(s) up to $300 (after first subtracting our standard NSF fee[s]). This will result in a negative Checking Account balance. The member will then have 30 days from the original date that the account went negative to make the required deposit(s) to bring the account positive.

Courtesy Pay is a <u>discretionary, noncontractual</u> (the member doesn't sign anything to receive or opt out) service. This service is offered to the members on a case-by-case situation and can be revoked at any time. Since this is a service designed to help members who inadvertently withdraw their account, members with excessive use of this service should be counseled on managing their checking account in a more responsible manner.

After ninety days, new checking accounts meeting the following criteria <u>will</u> be eligible for Courtesy Pay:

1. Open share draft (checking) suffix 9
2. Share draft (checking) open at least 90 days
3. No negative balances in any suffixes of more than $5.00
4. Primary member is at least 21 years of age
5. Deposits of at least $900.00 to share draft (checking) during the previous 90 days
6. Courtesy Pay field on member profile contains NA
7. Member code is not Org, House, Deceased, Escheat (funds in account are in the process of being transferred to the State as abandoned), BK, BK7, and BK13
8. Miscellaneous checking field does not contain ATM, Bad Address, BK, CCCS, CMS Collections, C/O, Code 4, Deceased, Does Not Qualify, Fraud, Negative, Opt Out, PIF, RTC, RTCK, Security, or TransWorld
9. Check Systems Field on MP does not contain Fail
10. No dormant restrictions
11. No loan delinquency of 15 days or more
12. Credit Card status on member profile does not contain: B, C, X, A, D, E, CO, CX, FO, EX, EO, E_, _X, _D, Z
13. "No Mail" field on member profile does not contain No Mail or Bad Address
14. NSF count on member profile cannot exceed 3 for current year

Courtesy Pay Removal Criteria

15. Negative balance in excess of $10.00 for 33 or more days
16. Negative balance in excess of $360.00
17. Courtesy Pay Notice returned as returned mail
18. Notice of bankruptcy filing
19. Deceased member notification
20. Closed account
21. Accounts in escheating process (funds in account are in the process of being transferred to the State as abandoned)
22. Security—Fraud—Garnishment on account

23. No loan delinquency of 45 days or more
24. Returned check notification
25. "Right to Cure" notification on any loan
26. CCCS/Debt management

Courtesy Pay Re-Qualification Criteria

27. Problem or issue surrounding Courtesy Pay program removal must be resolved
28. Initial Courtesy Pay criteria must be met starting from the date on which the problem/issue is resolved
29. Members who opted out may request reinstatement if the account meets inclusion criteria

Managers, Assistant Managers, or Coordinators may make exceptions as needed.